Next China-India War

World's First Water War-2029

Next China-India War

World's First Water War-2029

General S Padmanabhan
PVSM, AVSM, VSM (Retd)
Former Chief of the Army Staff, India

Manas Publications
(We Convert Fighters into Writers)
New Delhi-110002 (INDIA)

MANAS PUBLICATIONS
(Publishers for IAS, IPS, IFS, IRS, Defence, Press, Judges etc.)
(Publishers, Distributors, Importers & Exporters)
4402/5-A, Ansari Road (Opp. HDFC Bank)
Darya Ganj, New Delhi-110 002 (India)

Off: ✆ 011-23260783, 23265523, Res: 011-23842660
Fax: 011-23272766
E-mail: manaspublications@gmail.com
manaspublications@yahoo.com
Website: www.manaspublications.in

ISBN: 978-81-7049-499-7
₹ 795/-

Designed at
Manas Publications

Printed in India at
Printways, Delhi
and published by Mrs Suman Lata for
Manas Publications,
4402/5-A, Ansari Road, (Opp HDFC Bank),
Darya Ganj, New Delhi-110 002 (INDIA)

Dedication

This book is Dedicated to the Youth of India for it is on them that the future of our Country depends.

Preface

The Right to Life is guaranteed to its citizens by the Constitution of almost every country in the world. Water is a vital necessity for human beings to enable them to enjoy this constitutionally guaranteed right. However, these constitutions which guarantee life, do not guarantee availability of water. For that matter, the laws, conventions and the like which regulate life on this planet, do not guarantee that every life form on Earth will have access to the quantum of water it needs to sustain its life. What this serious omission might lead to is examined in this book.

From the dawn of History, civilizations have grown up on the banks of rivers. The names of the rivers Nile, Tigris, Euphrates, Indus, Ganges, and Mekong and so on readily come to mind. A significant commonality among these rivers is their transnational character, i.e. they originate in one country and flow through that country and a number of others before they enter the sea. The country in which the river originates is termed the 'Upper Riparian State' and the other countries through which the river flows are termed the 'Lower Riparian' States. As on date, international laws/conventions give the Upper Riparian State complete freedom on the utilization of the water of 'their' river, with only a pious appeal to them to respect the rights of other riparian states, The "Helsinki Rules, 1966" and the "UN Convention on the Law of the Non-Navigational Uses of International Water Courses, 1997," which constitute the body of the law on water use, have thus placed Lower Riparian States at the mercy of the Upper Riparian State— an entirely unacceptable position in a world of burgeoning population and dwindling water resources.

One country which is now posing an existential problem to India, Bangladesh and some other countries of South-East Asia is the People's Republic of China (PRC). PRC, exercising its 'right' as the Upper Riparian State, plans to divert the Brahmaputra river to flow from South to North instead of from North to South as it does now. This will deprive India's Ganges of nearly 40 per cent of its water and Bangladesh of even a greater percentage of water. And these two countries house well over a billion people! The law or convention which allows this is, without doubt, enabling PRC to 'steal' the waters of India and Bangladesh. In short, it is a 'bad' law which enables larceny and must be changed. Or, alternatively, the Upper Riparian State for the rivers originating in Tibet (as Brahmaputra is) should not be PRC whose 'Sino-centrism' is well known. Instead, Tibet, which was invaded and annexed by PRC, a dastardly act in which India pusillanimously, acquiesced when it recognized Tibet as a province of China, should be the Upper Riparian State. This will be possible as soon as Tibet regains her independence. As of now, India cannot trust the

Russia
Kazakhstan
Russia
Mongolia
Inner
Mongolia
Songhua
River
N. Korea
N
W
E
S
Beijing
Tianjin
Great Wall
PACIFIC
OCEAN
CHINA
Yellow River
Shanghai
India
Tibet
Yangtze
River
Nepal
Bhutan
India
Taipei
Taiwan
Guangzhou
Pearl River
Myanmar
Vietnam
Hong Kong
Macau
Hainan
SOUTH
CHINA SEA
Key
Water
River
Great Wall
City
Country border
map not to scale

fate of its millions of people to the greedy, self-serving PRC plan of South to North Diversion of the Brahmaputra. A free Tibet can, however, be relied on to take an appropriate decision which will satisfy all the riparian countries. In the words of Mr MS Menon, former Chief Engineer, Central Water Commission and Consultant on Water Resources, "Water is available to meet everybody's need, but not enough to meet their greed." One hopes Beijing is listening....

In this book, we shall be dealing with a possible scenario some 15 years hence by when PRC's fantastic development path would have plateaued out or may even have started dipping. By then, India, now on the rapid growth path, in consultation with many affected countries, takes steps to secure a more equitable Water Law and to restore Tibet its Independence and hence its status as the Upper Riparian State for all the rivers originating on the Tibetan highlands.

There may be more than a hint of hawkishness in this book. Doubts may arise whether all that follows is logical and likely to happen. Many ideas may seem to be overoptimistic even Utopian. If the Reader so feels, he should take up cudgels on behalf of South and South-East Asia and find a way to remove the peril of water larceny that is being planned by PRC in respect of the waters of Yarlung Tsangpo, our Brahmaputra.

General S. Padmanabhan (Retd)

Acknowledgements

I acknowledge with deep gratitude the inspiration and knowledge I have derived from the book "Water: Asia's New Battleground" by Mr Brahma Chellaney. His mastery of the subject and lucid way of expressing his thoughts make his book a 'MUST READ' for anyone dealing with the Water Problem that faces the World today. In extrapolating from the data provided by his book to the year 2029, I may have made numerous errors. I alone am responsible for these errors, omissions, distortions and some exaggerations.

My special thanks are due to my daughter Lakshmi for her great support in terms of very useful and timely research. I cannot thank her enough for typing out the entire manuscript, making numerous suggestions on both form and content to improve the overall tone of the book.

I am grateful to Manas Publications for encouraging me to write this book and patiently wait for it to reach their hands.

Finally, I thank my wife Roopa, who, despite her multifarious commitments, found time to listen to 'readings' from the book at odd hours and strengthening my resolve to complete the work I had undertaken.

Contents

Chapter 1

China: 2029-2030

Beijing, July 06, 2029

The sand storm blotted out visibility altogether. Such traffic as there was on the roads pulled off to the verges and awaited the passing of the storm with their headlights switched on. They had to wait till darkness fell for the storm to abate. However, the sand and dust that settled almost as snowflakes do, made any thought of driving home out of question as these formed a layer almost a metre high. People walked home or stayed in their cars in the stifling heat. 18 persons were reported to have choked to death in their cars by the dusty air. This was the fourth sand storm during the current week. All Beijing wondered whether they would ever see a normal day again. "What happened to our weather-control experts," they asked? "If they could prevent the rain from ruining the Opening Ceremony of the 2008 Beijing Olympics by seeding rain clouds likely to interfere on that Day of Glory for China, can they not keep the sand storms away?" they asked each other. Sadly the reply was the same: "Times have changed."

Shanghai, July 10, 2029

Xinhua News Agency quoting the Director of the Chinese Academy of Social Sciences stated that most of China endures choking smog, mass destruction of habitats and heavy metal poisoning of food articles. Water has become a critical problem throughout Northern China. The country as a whole uses about 400 cubic metres of water per person per year compared to about 1,600 cubic metres in USA. In Beijing water availability is a pitifully low 100 cubic metres per person per year—similar to what Saudi Arabia has. Water tables all over the country have dropped by about 250 to 300 metres since the 1970s. Half the rivers with significant catchment areas have simply 'disappeared' and what rivers have survived are being heavily polluted. The Yellow River (Huang Ho), a cradle of Chinese civilization, is heavily polluted. Since 1960 over 10,000 floating corpses have been recovered from the Yellow river. A survey carried out by the Yellow River Conservancy Commission some years ago surveyed 13,000 kilometres of the river and its tributaries. Its report stated that a third of the water is unfit even for agriculture—thanks to pollutants discharged by nearly 4,000 petrochemical plants built on its banks—and more such polluting industries are on the anvil. The report concluded with a sombre pronouncement, "In our quest for rapid industrial development and 'Great Power' status, we have polluted our rivers, nearly dried up sub-soil water and wrought havoc on our climate and the very air we breathe. Is there hope for redemption from the mess we are in?"

Tsinghua University, July 17, 2029

At a Seminar held in the University recently, there was near unanimity on the prodigal manner in which China had used its water resources. Total neglect of urban water infrastructure and unrealistic pricing of water in most cities was identified as a major cause. At the root of the populist pricing was the fear that the government would lose popularity! Comparing Chinese pricing of water with that of countries in Europe, the participants were appalled to find that whereas European countries levy approximately $ 60 per cubic metre of water, China charges only $ 8—a total mismatch between cost of production and revenue realization. The conclusion was inescapable—water pricing must be revisited; urban water infrastructure including pipes, treatment plants, reservoirs etc must be renewed on priority and, above all, polluting industries near waterways must be removed. Only then can China be saved—not by the Government's yen for gigantic dams and engineering projects, but by hardnosed attention to the basic problems of water pricing, infrastructure and management. Mr Sheng Wuchin, China's Minister for Water, in his concluding remarks stated, "Unless we learn to use the water that is already available prudently, it will be pointless for us to turn the Yarlung Tsangpo (Brahmaputra) from flowing South as ordained by Nature to flowing North as some people want to do. If we succeed in this mega effort, I can assure you we will waste the deviated river's water also."

Beijing, July 21, 2029

Voice of America quoting a reliable source reported that Mr Sheng Wuchin was arrested soon after the Tsinghua University Seminar on Water Problems in China, on July 17. He is likely to be charged with anti-Party activities. It may be recalled, the newscast continued, that Mr Sheng had come out with trenchant criticism of China's Water Policies which he inherited from his predecessors and was now responsible for implementing. The report added that Mr Sheng's remark that "the engineers who had ruled China for decades have brought the country to the brink of disaster where people have to fight for every drop of water" was considered enough for Mr Sheng to be put behind bars for many years.

Beijing, July 25, 2029

China's National People's Congress met in an extraordinary session over the last two days. Media were not invited to attend the proceedings. However, virtually everything that transpired during these two days was leaked out to the 'Media' by the Party members themselves! Clearly the 'leaks' were deliberate and meant to provide the Media with a 'sanitised' account of the proceedings and to reassure the country at large about matters of concern to them in their day-to-day life. The Beijing 'Foreign Journalists Club' issued a summary of the 'leaks' for the benefit of Chinese as well as World of Media. The summary is given on the next two pages.

Report on Extraordinary session of China's National People's Congress at Beijing on 23 and 24 July 2029

In the 'Review of the International and Internal Situation' Chinese leaders assessed that China was still regarded by USA, USSR and Europe as a 'Super Power'—this notwithstanding the decline in annual growth rate from over 8 per cent of GDP to a nominal 4 per cent now. The main reason for this decline was the drought from 2025 to 2027 which necessitated very heavy imports of food stuffs and a virtual collapse of their industries due to the flight of workers to their native places to undertake relief works for their families. In many areas, despite Government's best efforts, starvation deaths and outbreaks of gastro-enteric diseases in epidemic proportions took place; the latter due to the debilitated condition of the people aggravated by serious water pollution. "The situation is now under control. By early next year we hope to reach normalcy in both food grains availability and industrial production," the Premier said. He added, "The difficulties are not yet over. All of China must be prepared for major sacrifices to restore our great country to its Central status on the Planet as our name indicates."

He continued, "The 'sacrifices' required of the people have been spelt out in broad terms and would be explained and their implementation overseen by Party officials at every level—leaving the Government functionaries to attend to the organisation of relief and recovery work. The 'sacrifices' included cancellation of leave of all types, restriction of holidays to one day per month, extension of working hours to 16 hours per day with a half hour break after 8 hours and, to improve availability of man power, the drafting into the work force of all persons below the age of 70 years. The government also announced rationing of water for all those not actually working. Supply of electricity would be restricted to 8 hours per day, i.e. for four hours after dusk and four hours before dawn. Food grains will be rationed in such a manner as to ensure that workers are able to get 2,500 calories per day and others 1,800 calories. The implementation of rationing will be in the hands of the local body heads who should ensure full utilisation of local resources and avoid moving grains from far off places."

The Premier also announced that he has given the 'go-ahead' to the South to North Water Diversion Project (SNWD) under which the Yarlung Tsangpo will be diverted through canals and by tunnelling through mountain ranges to supply North-West China and the Beijing Area. He expressed the hope that those countries of South Asia who may be marginally affected by this diversion, will not create obstacles for this SNWD Project which, he said was "a life and death matter for North and North-West China."

Hangzou (East China), July 25, 2029

78, Beishan Street wore a festive look. The report received from Beijing about China's National People's Congress on 23 and 24 July was being discussed by international journalists who had flown out of Beijing to Hangzou where, at the Hangzou Hotel, an unscheduled meeting of the 'Foreign Correspondent's Club', Beijing, was in progress. None of the correspondents who were present, had any experience of the manner in which China faces its problems. To them it came as a deep shock to learn that the 'People's Republic' was as autocratic as Hitler's Germany or Mussolini's Italy in demanding extraordinary sacrifices of its people. There was near unanimity of views on the extremely hard schedule of work, absence of holidays and stringent control of rations. "Surely this sort of hardship is not ever imposed on one's own people in peace time" was the general opinion. Again the SNWD Project drew flak from most correspondents.

They recalled the solemn undertakings given by the then President of China Hu Jintao (2006) and later, Premier Wen Jiabao (Dec 2010) during their visits to Delhi that the SNWD Project was not being planned by China. Speculation was rife among the journalists as to what reactions there would be from India and Bangladesh to the SNWD Project and from other lower riparian countries like Myanmar (Salween river), Laos, Cambodia and Vietnam (Mekong river). The discussions concluded on a pessimistic note as the Doyen of the Foreign Journalists, Balwant S Bajwa of New Delhi Chronicle said, "Now we must get ready for War—possibly a War in which nuclear weapons may be used."

New Delhi, July 26, 2029

A spokesperson from the Ministry of External Affairs issued a brief statement to confirm that they are aware of the extraordinary meeting of the Chinese National People's Congress held at Beijing on 23-24 July. She said that the Chinese Ambassador in New Delhi had been asked to authenticate the fact of the Meeting, and to convey to our Government the Chinese position with regard to the South to North Water Diversion Project in relation to the Brahmaputra river or the Yarlung Tsangpo as it is called in the Tibetan language. The need for utmost urgency in obtaining authoritative version of the Chinese position in the matter was stressed. The spokesperson also stated that the Government of India was in close touch with the Governments of friendly countries of South and South East Asia who will also be affected by any Chinese decision on the SNWD Project.

Pasighat (Arunachal Pradesh), India, July 26, 2029

A radio message received from a Border Roads

Organisation (BRO) Road Maintenance Patrol from the area of Guyor La on the McMahon Line as received at the BRO Company HQ at Pasighat reads: "Party on patrol in area Guyor La found tell-tale marks of Chinese military movement in that area (.) some cigarette butts and one packet of Chinese cigarettes, a partly filled bottle of water and a broken pair of cutting pliers of Chinese make retrieved from the area(.) examination of the tree on which India's Lion Emblem is nailed revealed that the pliers apparently broke when attempt was made to remove the metal plate on which our insignia is marked (.) border NOT repeat NOT crossed by the Chinese (.) own helicopter seen flying at 1145 hrs today on own side LAC towards Kasi Nala (.) all well (.) Jai Hind."

Itanagar (Arunachal Pradesh), July 27, 2029

Chief Minister of Arunachal Pradesh in response to a question in the State Assembly said that constant vigil is being maintained along the LAC by the Para-Military Forces, Police and the State Intelligence Personnel. Every hamlet and village in the state has been asked to redouble their vigil over tracks/paths through hills and report any unusual sighting to the nearest Police Post/Para Military Force Command Post. So far, there was nothing unusual except for a report of tampering with the Indian marker on the LAC at Guyor La yesterday.

...

Chapter-2

Resurgent India: 2029

New Delhi, July 27, 2029

The Ram Lila Grounds, a chosen venue for very large or very important meetings, was simply stated, a sea of humanity. The occasion was the first anniversary of the liberation of the Northern Territories which had been under Pakistan's occupation since 1947-48 and the freeing of the long-suffering people of Gilgit-Skardu by Indian Forces. Above all, the Indian actions severed the road communication between China and Pakistan via Occupied Tibet. As a feat of arms and demonstration of the enormous capability achieved in joint Army-IAF operations, the occasion was historic. For the first time in the history of warfare, over 25,000 Indian troops had carried out high altitude air-borne-cum-air-landed operations supported by land based guns and rocket artillery using special enhanced-effect ammunition. The entire operation was carried out over a 24 hour period including the laying down of arms by a Pakistani force supported by a Chinese regiment ex 13th Combined Corps (Chengdu Military Region). Our casualties were minimal for an operation of this magnitude—7 officers and 23 soldiers—killed or wounded. Of these 30 casualties, 8 proved fatal even after treatment at the Base Hospital. The Pak and PLA casualties too were minimal due to the numbing shock of the air attacks preceded by the devastating long range rocket and artillery fire. 1,600 soldiers ex Pak Army and 360 ex PLA were taken PoW. It was certainly a victory to celebrate for all-India and not only the Armed Forces.

Speaking to the vast audience assembled in the Ram Lila Grounds, Prime Minister Mr Jagannath Das spoke of the tremendous progress India had made since the time India was economically debilitated following an all-world monetary crisis and a few very bad monsoon seasons. What brought us through the grim days was the grit and stamina of our young Indians—they, more than any change of Government or foreign aid were the architects of India's transformation from being a 'developing' country to a country which had re-written all the texts of political systems, governance and national economy and in the process had become the largest economy in the world. Mr Das said, "I saw a sea-change come over our youth. Instead of lining up outside Employment Exchanges and waiting for someone to give them work, they got together in groups of varying sizes and took on every manner of work ranging from very high technology work to more pedestrian tasks. Our Banks drew inspiration from their 'Self Belief' and advanced whatever funds they required without following the laid down procedures. It was fantastic to see the Banks thus trusting our young generation and being rewarded by achievements of great magnitude by the youth and greater earnings for the Banks. In fact, if India has achieved a huge quantum jump in its scientific, industrial, financial, health and infrastructure sectors as it, indeed, has, the credit must go to these young men and women—mostly under 30 years of age. They also formed groups to boost agricultural production and dairy farming. All in all, I am here today to salute the true heroes of Modern India, our Youth." (Sustained cheering.)

Continuing his speech Mr Das said, "China has once again decided to revive the South to North Water Diversion Project in respect of the Brahmaputra or, as it is called across the Himalayas, Yarlung Tsangpo. We have told them categorically that we shall not allow this project to be undertaken as its completion will starve us and Bangladesh for water. This will affect our agriculture to the extent of our losing 40 per cent of our food grain produce and Bangladesh of 70 per cent or so. The ecological price we shall have to pay will also be terribly high—from riverine fish to large mammals like cattle, rhinocerii and elephants—all life forms will be affected. I do not wish to alarm you, but I must say this very clearly and loudly—the Water Diversion Project will be resisted by us with all our might; it shall not be allowed by us." There was complete silence at the Ram Lila Grounds as the Prime minister concluded his address. Perhaps for half a minute, everyone conjured up mental images of the portent the Prime Minister's remarks conveyed. And then, starting with a few hundred people echoing the Prime Minister's words, "It shall not be allowed by us," a huge tsunami of voices took up the cry "We shall not allow it." The clamour was so great that one might imagine even the Chinese in Beijing hearing it! And they did—by radio and television they heard and saw millions of Indians unitedly telling them not to even think of diverting the Brahmaputra—and their top leaders were cold with fear. They knew the military might of India of 2029 would outfight their PLA—unless, and here is when the fear rose to a peak—unless nuclear weapons were used. But then India too was nuclear armed and a fight with nuclear weapons between the two most populated nations on Earth would mean Armageddon.

Beijing, July 26, 2029, 0530 hrs (Local Time)

The top leadership of PRC met at the Presidential Residence in the former 'Imperial City'. A cool breeze blowing from the lake perhaps helped the leaders to face the emergency that had necessitated this meeting in a reasonably calm manner. This was a far cry from the agitation that the live telecast from the Ram Lila Grounds had evoked from them. President Hong and Premier Lung met separately in the study initially. They agreed that a very delicate situation had been created by the Indian response to their taking up work on the SNWD Project. To 'wriggle' out of it would be impossible as it will cause them to lose face. It will be equally bad if not worse if they inform New Delhi of their intention to go ahead with the Project and start work. The result of this will be, inevitably, a New Delhi referral of the matter to the UNO and a simultaneous mobilization of Indian forces to forestall any attempt on our part to go ahead with the Project. This dilemma was discussed at length and a decision was taken that there would be no backing out of the decision to go ahead with the SNWD Project; however, they would offer to hold discussions with India on how to reduce to the minimum the adverse effect of the Project on India and so schedule the Project work so as to allow the Indians adequate time to make alternative arrangements for the water they will have to lose. President Hong, though not fully convinced by the offer to hold discussions, said, "We do not have a choice. India is too strong for us to take her on militarily unless we use nuclear weapons. This would lead to great mutual destruction and possibly embroil the whole world. Yet, we must try it." Premier Lung was asked to make the offer to discuss the SNWD Project with India either in Beijing or at New Delhi and arrive at a mutually acceptable solution. The Premier said that China could offer to compensate India to the extent of loss of agricultural produce due to the diversion and supply free electricity to the extent of half a million kilowatts in addition, provided the transmission lines and other arrangements to carry this quantum of electricity to Indian Power Grid were made by India. This offer of free electricity will be valid for a period of 10 years from the time SNWD Project succeeds in turning Yarlung Tsangpo northwards.

Since no other viable course of action short of dropping the Project could be found, Premier Lung was directed to make his offer to India as discussed. He was also asked to work out a similar compensation package for Bangladesh and deal with the offer and negotiations as a tri-partite issue rather than a Sino-Indian issue. The meeting ended on an optimistic note as a Muslim League dominated Bangladesh could spike India's guns as it were and give China more room for manoeuvre. The meeting ended four hours after it started.

Baroda House, New Delhi, July 31, 2029, 1100 hrs

The Indian and Bangladesh delegates for the tri-partite meeting convened at China's request to discuss their plan to divert the waters of the Brahmaputra river (Yarlung Tsangpo) from flowing South to flowing North were already in the Conference Hall with their entourage. Both Indian and Bangladeshi delegates were led by respective ministers for Water, Irrigation and Power. The Indian team was led by Mr Tirumalai Iyengar, a former head of the

Central Water and Power Commission and considered a legend among dam builders in India. The Bangladesh team was led by Mr Shahid ul Alam, again an Engineer of repute. The two leaders spent about 30 minutes together before the Chinese delegation arrived and co-ordinated their stand on the Chinese proposals which had been e-mailed to them by 1600 hrs the previous day.

The Chinese delegation arrived at the venue at 1145 hrs and after exchange of pleasantries the meeting started with a brief address by Mr Liu Bijiam, China's Minister for Water and Power. After thanking India for hosting the meeting and Bangladesh for also attending the meeting, he said:

> "My country has a population of 1.3 billion people, in other words, 22 per cent of the World's population. They need a lot of water, specially clean, potable water for drinking and cooking. Unfortunately we have only 8 per cent of the fresh water supply of the World. We have exploited virtually every fresh water source in our country—rivers, springs, lakes, glacial melts and subsoil water to unimaginable depths. Yet, North-Western parts of China are turning into deserts for want of water. It is to prevent desertification of NW China and to recharge the Yellow River (Hwang Ho) that we have conceived the project of South to North Water Diversion of the Yarlung Tsangpo. By executing this project, China hopes to bring relief to the thirsty millions of people of NW China and stave off the spectre of desertification. We are aware that completion of this project will have some adverse effects on both India and Bangladesh as the inflow into India will be reduced to some extent; so also the flow of these waters to Bangladesh. We are aware that this will affect your agriculture, wild life, fisheries, river navigability and, in the case of Bangladesh, salinity of the delta areas. We have factored all this into our plans

> and are prepared to consider a suitable compensation package for India as well as Bangladesh. The details of the package in terms of compensation for notional crop loss, ecological damage and so on can be worked out jointly by us once you—India and Bangladesh—agree to withdraw your opposition to SNWD Project. I thank you for your courteous attention. We may now discuss the technical issues involved and their likely impact on your countries—both adverse and beneficial in terms of freedom from annual flood havoc. Thank you."

The Chinese delegation leader Mr Liu was smiling as he resumed his seat after his clear cut enunciation of the necessity for the SNWD Project and its likely effects on India and Bangladesh and the readiness of the Chinese to compensate for the ill effects. The smile disappeared soon after the Indian Delegation leader Mr Tirumalai Iyengar began to speak. Mr Tirumalai Iyengar stood up to speak next. He said,

> "Hon'ble Mr Liu Bijian and members of the Chinese delegation. We have just been entertained to a remarkably insensitive speech on the SNWD Project. Mr Liu's fluency and smooth talk of compensation packages reminded me of our river Brahmaputra, whose waters Mr Liu wants to take away so that the NW part of his country may flourish even as the NE part of our country and all of Bangladesh suffer great hardship. Mr Liu talked of 'compensation'; it was like throwing a few pieces of bread at a barking dog so that it may stop barking. Mr Liu, India and Bangladesh are not 'barking' for your petty crumbs. We are faced by a most serious existential problem which your diversion of the waters of the Brahmaputra will entail. The problem we might have to face is 'Will we live or die?' Mr Liu, I shall request you to return to your country and inform your leaders that under no circumstances

> shall we allow you to carry out the SNWD Project. You may also add my personal observation that the Brahmaputra is not a household water pipe, which can be turned on or off by he who has control over the tap. Brahmaputra is the carotid artery or jugular vein if you wish to call it, of India and Bangladesh. You will not be allowed to tamper with it. Should you try to do so, we shall snatch the 'tap' from your hands so that you may not cause further nuisance to the countries of this region. Thank you for listening patiently."

There was absolute silence after this very aggressive talk by Mr Iyengar. Taking advantage of it, the Bangladesh delegation leader Mr Shahid ul Alam rose and said, "Bangladesh stands shoulder to shoulder with India on the SNWD Project. We shall not allow it—compensation or no compensation. Thank you."

Chinese Embassy, New Delhi, July 31, 2029

In the face of the blunt replies given by the Indian and Bangladesh Delegation Leaders, Mr Liu and the rest of his delegation did the only thing they could possibly do, i.e. bow austerely to their host and walk out of Baroda House to their waiting cars. They drove to the Chinese Embassy and communicated what had transpired at the meeting to the Ambassador and then on a secure telephone connection to the Chinese Premier Mr Lung. The Premier conveyed to President Hong the total refusal of India and Bangladesh to any arrangement arrived at allowing the SNWD Project to proceed unhindered and suggested that an urgent meeting of the top leadership including the military and the Party be convened at the earliest to take stock of the situation and formulate a suitable course of action. Mr Hong concurred with this suggestion and directed the Premier to return immediately to Beijing and order a meeting of the Central Committee of the Party on 8th August.

Prime Minister's Office, New Delhi, July 31, 2029

The Cabinet Committee on Security met in an emergency session at 1800 hrs. Apart from the normal members of the committee, Mr Tirumalai Iyengar was invited to attend. The meeting started with a brief resume by the National Security Advisor of the security situation including that arising out of our turning down the Chinese offer to compensate us in return for our agreeing to the SNWD Project. The Prime Minister Mr Jagannath Das asked Mr Tirumalai Iyengar to give his assessment of how soon the Chinese may be able to start the Project and when we might be confronted with a 'north-flowing' Brahmaputra.

Mr Iyengar gave a resume of the meeting that morning and the stunned expression on the Chinese faces when both Bangladesh and we rejected their offer. Apparently, they expected that we would have no choice but to agree and may have moved plant and machinery to appropriate places for starting the Project in anticipation of our agreement. In fact, whether we agreed to their proposal or not, they had made up their mind to execute the SNWD Project and may be ready to start even within a week! The Project had been worked out in detail almost a year or so ago and necessary surveys had been conducted for all the three routes by which the waters of various rivers are to be diverted northwards. These routes are:

a. Eastern Route. To transfer water from the Yangtse to Tianjin in the North. It involves burrowing a tunnel beneath the Yellow River and expanding the 1,000 km Grand Canal into the longest aqueduct in the world. It does not involve the Brahmaputra though it is part of the SNWD Project. Partly completed.

b. Central Route. Again this is part of the SNWD Project but does not involve the Brahmaputra.

c. Western Route. This involves transfer of water of the Brahmaputra, the Salween (or Nu in Chinese), the Mekong (Lancang in Chinese) and the Jinsha (a major tributary of the Yangtse). The plan calls for a series of canals and tunnels over a route of 1,215 km in Eastern Tibet, connecting the upper reaches of the Yangtse to that of the Yellow River—again by tunnels and canals some 300 km long in the earthquake prone Bayankala Mountains. The Project may be completed by mid 2050 or even later with the maximum time being spent on tunnelling and working in earthquake prone areas.

"The point I am making here," said Mr Iyengar is that the Western route being the most difficult and involving collection of water from a number of rivers including the Brahmaputra, may be taken up in a phased manner—Mekong and the Salween have been fairly well dammed and the Brahmaputra must, therefore, be the next in line to be dammed—exactly where, we are not aware. However these dams will be storage oriented and not run-of-the-river type used for power generation alone. They would, therefore, take away waters from the Brahmaputra based on their storage capacity, which, when tunnels/canals to connect northwards are ready, will be feeding these. These, therefore, are likely to be built first—probably disguised as run-of-the-river power projects. They may start within this year or early in 2030 keeping in mind that the entire SNWD Project is to be completed by 2050. My advice as an engineer is that if the initial dams on the Brahmaputra are not allowed to be built, the SNWD Project will lose its importance and may even be abandoned."

Considerable discussion of the views of Mr Iyengar took place and finally, the NSA summed up the issues involved and said that China will resist physical interference at various dam sites militarily and that unless these sites are denied to the Chinese by pre-emptive action of some nature, it may become very difficult for us to stop the SNWD Project taking effect. This was further discussed and the decisions as under were taken:

a R & A W to endeavour to pinpoint the sites where the Chinese intend to dam the Brahmaputra. Own hydro-engineers to cooperate.

b Contingency plans to be worked out for prevention of the building of these dams or, if any are built, for their destruction.

c Specially trained Tibetan Military Personnel to be tasked to further the intelligence acquisition effort and to locate the areas where tunnels are to be dug using low yield nuclear explosives.

d While all the above will be planned and executed to a point short of hostile action all out diplomatic efforts will be made to pressurize China to abandon the SNWD Project—specially the Western route which affects all of South and South East Asia.

Mr Tirumalai Iyengar was thanked for rebuffing the Chinese attempt to secure our consent for the SNWD Project and excused from the meeting which continued after a half hour break with a reduced version of the CCS. The Prime Minister, External Affairs Minister, Defence Minister, Finance Minister, National Security Adviser, and the Chief of Defence Staff formed this core group. The Prime Minister said that he will enunciate a number of plans and would like the reactions of concerned officers to these at their next session at 0900 hrs on 1st August at his residence on Race Course Road.

Chapter-3

Consultations

7, Race Course Road, New Delhi, August 1, 2029, 0900 hrs

The conference was held in the residence of the Prime Minister instead of in the large conference room at No 7 RCR. The mini-conference Room in the PM's residence was adequate for 16 persons and since only 6 persons were attending, this was ample. The greatest advantage it had over 7RCR was that the informal atmosphere helped overcome inhibitions and one could speak what was in one's mind freely. Suitable refreshments had been placed near each attendee and there would be no need to call any house staff in for this purpose.

The PM chatted with the attendees about everything but the business on hand for a while. The topic which involved everyone in animated conversation was the 3D version of a popular Hindi movie which all of them had seen some 15 years ago. After a bit of this, the PM called the meeting to order.

The first proposal the PM made was about Tibet. He said, "Tibet was never a part of China. Ethnically, culturally, by religious persuasion and historically, they have little in common with PRC. Even after the British left and we became independent, Tibet was regarded as a free country. We had our mission at Lhasa, trade missions at Yatung and Shigatse. Unfortunately, after the Communists won control over China, they took energetic steps to secure the area beyond their frontiers. Tibet was one such area. After India (like the British before them) accepted the suzerainty of China over Tibet, they began to treat the Tibetans as second class citizens. The Chinese are predominantly of 'Han' stock and they looked down on the Tibetans. From mocking at their lifestyle, religion and backwardness, they descended to the level of treating Tibetans as vassals. Among the Tibetans is a tribe known as 'Khampa'. They are warlike, fearless and sensitive to being exploited. The Khampas rose in rebellion against the Han Chinese in an unorganized manner and with primitive weapons like swords, bows and arrows and an occasional spear. They were crushed by China and a large number were killed and many fled to India. The Chinese reportedly planned to eliminate the Dalai Lama who is treated as God incarnate by the Tibetans. To save his life, the Khampas and a number of other Tibetans fled with the Dalai Lama to India where he resides till today with a Tibetan Government-in-exile. Unfortunately, India was bent upon supporting the PRC.

At their request and to foster good relations between us and PRC, we recognized Tibet as a province of China. It was an indefensible decision of our government at that time, one which acquiesced in the exploitation of a free people and the cause of much trouble to not only Tibet, but also India and South East Asia. This is so as it gave China the right as the Upper Riparian country to control the waters of the numerous rivers including the Indus, Brahmaputra, Salween, and Mekong to her advantage and the detriment of all other lower riparians."

My proposal is this: If Tibet were recognised by us as an independent country and free of Chinese yoke, she becomes the Upper Riparian country—a duty which, with her well established cultural practices, she would discharge with consideration for all other riparian countries. I am aware that we shall be trying to turn the clock back as it were when we recognize Tibet's Independence. But, didn't we do much the same in the case of erstwhile East Bengal, which was then a part of Pakistan and whose people revolted against the reprehensible treatment they received from Pakistan? I propose that we correct the historical blunder we made six decades ago and recognize Tibet as a sovereign nation and NOT a part of China. Please examine the implication of this move from all possible angles and revert back to me one week from now on 8th August. Please ensure that your discussions with your teams and the intended steps to recognize Tibetan freedom are not prematurely leaked.

The next area where I wish to seek your views and a concrete plan to implement the decision we may arrive at relates to the oppressed people living in other countries contiguous to China and seeking their right to be free of Chinese domination. I have in mind the Uyghurs of Eastern Turkestan and Inner Mongolia. While the former rebelled earlier too, they were ruthlessly crushed by the Chinese. The latter were actually a part of the Republic of Mongolia and were handed over by the Russians when they vacated Inner Mongolia to China instead of, as logic suggests, to Outer Mongolia. How can we convert these two issues to our advantage? Once again, consider for a week and revert to me.

The next issue I wish to have your views on is freedom of navigation in the South China Sea. You are aware of the good work done by our ONGC Videsh Limited in cooperation with Petro Vietnam in certain specified blocks in the South China Sea. This was objected to by China which claimed the South China Sea was a Chinese domain. Our movements to/from Vietnam are being shadowed ominously by Chinese vessels. So far, there has been no overt interference with our movements there, but with our recent rebuff to the Chinese on the SNWD Project, it is likely that some incident may be engineered by the Chinese against our ships in South China Sea. Though Vietnam is wholly supportive of our actions, I consider that an Indian Naval presence in those waters may have a calming effect on the hot heads of the Chinese. I would like the Chief of Defence Staff to examine what I have said and advise Government on the best method to stymie the Chinese in South China Sea. Kindly discuss this matter after a week during which we may also be able to judge whether our recent anti-SNWD Project stance has caused any ripples in the South China Sea.

One last point—and perhaps the most delicate of all that I have outlined: "We have left the Chinese free to do what they want everywhere. Even the USA does not worry them if they carry out brutalities in Tibet or Xinjiang or in Nei Monggol. All three areas must be visited by an India 'proxy'. We have conducted special training for volunteers from each of these three areas and I understand they are up to 'special forces' standards. If we can assist them in training, we should not quail at providing them data for target selection in their native areas. With our widespread coverage from our military satellites as well as information obtained from our intelligence agents abroad, we should be able to direct some of the India-trained personnel to sensitive Chinese targets in these areas. To paraphrase and twist what their late lamented Chairman Mao said in October 1962 '...since the Chinese stick their heads out and insist on fighting our friends, for us not to create trouble for them would not be friendly enough. Courtesy emphasizes reciprocity—even though it may be by proxy.' I am certain our CDS would attend to this proposal as well."

Prime Minister's Office, South Block, New Delhi, August 3, 2029

The Permanent Representative of India at the United Nations Organisation arrived at New Delhi Airport at dawn and after a refreshing ice water bath and changing into India friendly clothes, arrived at the PMO at 1000 hrs as required. Mr Arun K Roy or AK as he is generally addressed was ushered into the PM's office immediately. The PM got up to shake his hand and move to the sofa arrangement on one side of the large room. He said, "Thank you for coming over at short notice, AK; we are trying to create some more interesting work for you."

"Delighted to hear that Sir. My only complaint about the UN is that it is very boring as everyone who is anyone seems to be perpetually delivering a speech."

"Well, I can cure that with a few words. You see AK, we have got totally fed up with the Chinese who are constantly creating problems for us and our South-East Asian friends. Now, they want to divert the Brahmaputra river which flows south into India from Tibet at Tuting and make it flow towards the north and north-west part of their country. They may have to dig canals right across Tibet and use nuclear explosives to blast their way through some intervening mountains. They hope to complete this North to South Diversion of the Brahmaputra (which they call Yarlung Tsangpo) in about 20 years—say by 2050. They asked us and Bangladesh, the two countries which will be most affected by this project to accept a compensation package to make up our losing 40 per cent and Bangladesh over 60 per cent of our water. We have refused categorically. We need to take this up in the UN and prevent the diversion of our Brahmaputra."

AK seemed a bit shocked. He said, "How can they divert our river? I know Brahmaputra originates near Lake Mansarovar in Tibet and that China is, therefore, the Upper Riparian country, yet this project seems to be very inconsiderate of other riparians. I think we can argue this out in the UN but what if the UN refuses to stop China from undertaking this Project on the grounds that the Upper Riparian State can use the river in whatever manner it wishes to? I believe that China has sovereign 'riparian rights' over the river as per the doctrine of prior appropriation."

"Now AK, do not quote the law as it stands, but, instead look holistically at the problem differently—as one which will benefit one large country which is not at present using the river and deprive two very populous countries which are using the river's water for their very existence. Surely, the doctrine of prior appropriation is being misused!"

"I have no doubt, Sir, that what you say is just and can be argued out but as it stands, the Law favours the Upper Riparian, China," said AK, "unless, unless...."

"AK, you have zeroed in on the essential weakness in the law—the Helsinki Rules, 1966 which is what I will call the 'basic' international water law, was written when Tibet, by right of conquest by China and our own folly, came under this law for the first time. If we can go back to, say 1950 or so, when Tibet was an unconquered country, they would have enjoyed the advantage of the 'Doctrine of

Prior Appropriation' and full rights as the Upper Riparian State. I am having this aspect examined by the Ministry of Law and I hope they will agree with my views. If they do, I shall withdraw our recognition of Tibet as a province of China and persuade as many South and South-East Asian countries to support us—hopefully we will then have a more sensible and judicious Upper Riparian who will ensure that we might all get our due—even China!"

"That will be a very bold step, Sir, and I believe it may work if we present our case with thorough preparation. If you permit, I shall spend a few days with the Ministry of Law and keep myself fully in the picture" said AK.

"That is what I want you to do. If our move does not succeed, we can join Dickens and say...Law is such an ass."

Prime Minister's Office, New Delhi, August 8, 2029

The Prime Minister greeted the Chief of Defence Staff with a cheerful "Good to see you General Gyani" and waved him to a chair. "The National Security Adviser will be here shortly and we can then discuss what you have come to tell me." Even as he spoke Mr Nambiar, formerly of the IFS and now National Security Adviser, entered the office and took a chair next to the CDS.

"Well Gentlemen, what is the result of your efforts over the last week on the matters I had raised?" he said.

Speaking first, Nambiar said, "Sir, we have carefully considered the question of our supporting, by covert or overt operations, the Uyghurs, Inner Mongols and the Tibetans. We have also considered the question of creating a naval presence in the South China Sea to check any wayward action by the Chinese. CDS will briefly outline the proposed actions. Over to him, Sir."

Speaking in a calm, measured tone, Gen Gyani said, "We have a readymade situation available in Kashgar, Xinjiang. There have been, for some considerable time, bad blood between the Uyghurs and the Tungans—the name Uyghurs have given to the Chinese Muslims. Tungans have been exploiting the Uyghurs (who are also Muslims) in many ways like dispossessing them of their land or house or shop or making them work in their households as unpaid servants. They are pro-Han and very anti-Uyghur. From time to time, incidents have occurred in which Uyghurs have retaliated against the Tungan and suffered reprisals as a result. Over a period of time, a number of Uyghur notables have gone into the mountains near the Pamir Plateau where they have formed an anti-Tungan, anti-Chinese movement whose aim is to win freedom for Uyghurs so that they may once again attempt union with Turkestan or Kazakhstan. So far, we have cultivated a few of the separatist leaders and have trained a number of their personnel. Their capacity is at present limited to hit and run raids on Tungan areas, ambushing Chinese vehicles and generally being a nuisance. As of now, I think we should improve their fighting capabilities and use them as a readymade resistance group to harass and cause damage to the Chinese when we are at or close to war with them. Their own cause of union with Turkestan or Kazakhstan, I am afraid, is unlikely to prosper. So we shall have to reward them in some other way when the time comes—maybe by opening a modern hospital, establishing educational facilities and so on. For your information, Sir, we have a 'point-man' at Urumqi—the Xinjiang capital and occasionally we meet him somewhere in one of the Central Asian countries. For the present, however, we may not task the Uyghurs beyond their present capability."

The PM was clearly impressed by what he had heard. He said, "That was a very lucid account of the Uyghurs and their problems and capabilities. I agree with you that we must wait for an opportune moment for tasking them more heavily. Nambiar, you agree with that 'wait to task' approach?" Nambiar laughed and said, "Yes Sir. That will be the wisest course."

Continuing his briefing of the Prime Minister, Gen Gyani said, "Regarding the Inner Mongol or, as the Chinese call them 'Nei Monggol', it is worth recalling that Mongolia was never a part of China till a decade after the collapse of the Manchu Empire in 1911. The Outer Mongols (also called Khalkha Mongol) then struggled for a full decade against the remnants of the Manchu Empire and proclaimed their independence as People's Republic of Mongolia. Inner Mongolia was unable to unite with them as it was held in the stranglehold of Chinese warlords. However, under the leadership of a direct descendent of Genghis Khan, Prince De Wang, an Inner Mongol, succeeded in raising an army and ruling Inner Mongolia almost as a self-governing territory till 1945. In 1945, the Soviet Union, jointly with the Mongol Army, forced the Japanese to vacate China. It was at this stage that Inner Mongolia was transferred by the Soviets to their new protégé PRC. Since then, Inner Mongolia has been a region of China, suffering periodic pogroms which resulted in the killing of a tenth part of their population and the virtual takeover of most of their pasture lands by Han Chinese and the indignity of being treated as second class citizens. Our estimate is that given suitable encouragement, means and training, Inner Mongolia could be used to tie down some PLA troops to maintain law and order. I do not foresee any great contribution from them against China as they have, over the last six decades, been bludgeoned into a submissive people devoted to animal husbandry and the unenviable position of being the most backward region of China. For the present, I do not recommend any major role being assigned to Inner Mongolia against China."

"That is sad—particularly so as it is the native place of the 'Great' or Terrible' Genghis Khan. But a subjugated and totally suppressed Inner Mongolia may not be an asset to us in our future plans. Not with standing this, we should keep track of what goes on in that part of China so that we may convert any fleeting opportunity into a significant gain for our cause. I think, Nambiar, you should have a meeting with Rathore, Secretary RAW regarding this."

The CDS continued his briefing. He said, "I shall now go on to the most promising region of China where we have excellent opportunity to more than severely embarrass—in fact decisively defeat the Chinese militarily as well as politically. In our favour and against the Chinese are a number of elements. First is the Tibetan Government in Exile functioning from India with complete control over all Tibetans in Tibet, India or anywhere else due to the great moral and religious authority of His Holiness, the Dalai Lama. The people of Tibet will support us in any activity which has been cleared by him. We must keep in mind, of course, as a 'God Incarnate' we must not expose His Holiness to anything which is offensive to him on any ground whatever. He is the key to victory over the Chinese in Tibet."

The Prime Minister interjected, "Unlike the late Joseph Stalin who, when asked to encourage Catholicism in USSR in order to conciliate the Pope, I shall not ask the Pope how many divisions he has got. The Dalai Lama's influence is far greater than that of a whole army when it comes to action in Tibet. We must always see that whatever we do has his blessings—but, I am interrupting. Please continue, General."

"Other factors in our favour are that a very large number of Tibetan youth have been trained by us in warfare in high altitude areas and clandestine operations. We have been able to familiarize a fair number of them with Tibetan terrain and climatic conditions—in fact almost 10 per cent of Tibetans born in India during the last twenty years have been able to visit Tibet, of course, unofficially. Knowledge of the terrain and the vulnerabilities of the Chinese army of occupation—like nodal points of the road system, railways and fuel pipelines, location of troops' barracks, storage areas for food and ammunition of various types are a few of these which our Tibetans have studied during their visits home. They have also been able to 'size up' the Chinese soldiers during these visits."

"The most important factor that will work in our favour in Tibet is that the Tibetan fighting alongside us will be totally charged with patriotic fervour whereas his opponents, the Chinese soldiers will be low on morale—fighting in a far away land where the people hate them. Keeping these advantages that are clearly perceived by us for operations in Tibet, we propose intensification of high altitude warfare training, air-borne operations in high altitudes, careful study of high definition satellite imagery of vulnerable points in Tibet and constantly updating ourself on the Chinese road/rail communication systems, dumps of warlike stores and accommodation of Chinese troops—locations, numbers, security systems and so on. Broadly the employment of Tibetans will be in the form of battalion groups, each having three or four Companies, mortars, an affiliated artillery battery, a forward air controller to call for air support and 10 to 12 animals for carriage of ammunition, reserves, rations and special communication equipment. We should task them initially on objectives within two days march from the border. Later, when the Chinese are destabilized or are 'on the run', they will form the spearhead for entry into Lhasa and other cities/towns on the Xinjiang-Tibet Highway. Apart from these troops, commandos of the Tibetan Special Forces, the equivalent of two Indian SF Battalions will be assigned special tasks from before D-Day and continuously thereafter for a variety of tasks which it is not necessary to specify just yet. To sum up, Tibetan troops will be employed both independently and alongside

Indian troops. For better coordination, each Indian Brigade will have a Tibetan Liaison Group of suitable size. For mobility, skis/tracked snow vehicles of 1 tonne capacity and standard Indian B vehicles will be made available to the Tibetan force. So much for the present, Sir. We shall be able to brief you closer to the time on operational plans in the Army Operations Room."

The Prime Minister, who had been nodding approval at regular intervals while Gen Gyani was speaking, now walked up to the general and said, "Gyani, Tibet must be free again—politically, culturally and to choose their leaders. We must deal with them as equal comrades and see that their fight for the liberation of their country is successful. I rely on you to achieve this. Let us take a short break while I meet our Chief Justice who is retiring today from the stewardship of the Supreme Court. We shall meet again in, say, 15 minutes—so do not go away."

On the return of the Prime Minister, Gen Gyani resumed: Regarding the question of Chinese adventurism in the South China Sea against Indian ships, there should not be any Chinese interference with them under the United Nations Convention on the Law of the Sea (UNCLOS). The United States has, in the past, carried out manoeuvres in the South China Sea on the plea that 'peaceful surveillance and other military activities may be carried out in a country's EEZ without permission' under the UNCLOS—even though the USA is not a member of this Convention! My belief is that the Chinese will not, similarly, challenge our right to move about in the South China Sea. We saw instances of their reluctance to start any trouble with our Naval ships as was the case with *INS Airavat* in July 2011 and in June 2012 when a PLA Navy frigate shadowed Indian Navy vessels for 12 hours while they were in the South China Sea. This is not to rule out any 'misbehaviour' on the part of the Chinese. They have a propensity for autocratism and have, in the past, issued decrees such as declaring a 'No Fly Zone' over an uninhabited island disputed with Japan and, more recently, requiring foreign vessels to seek a permit from Chinese regional authorities for carrying out surveys of any kind, fishing etc in the South China Sea. We should not allow our ships to be so tied down as we have UNCLOS to back us and if there is any harassment of our ships, moving a strong flotilla of a 'few' IN ships to defy these orders. We hope such a policy of the South China Sea being treated by us as a genuinely free zone for world shipping will be highly appreciated by the SE Asian countries. The same kind of treatment—but with IN aircraft or IAF aircraft—should be used to cure the Chinese of the ridiculous fixation with 'no fly zones' and so on. We should be able to handle these issues by adopting a firm policy backed up by adequate force as the South China Sea is one of the busiest shipping routes in the world. Besides, if and when we have to engage China in hostilities, this area will be very important for us to dominate. For this purpose, we should increase Naval visits to our friends in the South China Seas area and abutting it, i.e. Vietnam, Philippines, Brunei, Malaysia and so on."

"Thank you Gyani, for a clear enunciation of the South China Sea issue. It is a very important area for commercial shipping without doubt. However, its importance will increase exponentially as oil and natural gas sources are fully surveyed and exploited. USA estimates oil reserves of 28 billion barrels while the corresponding Chinese figure is 213 billion barrels. Similarly natural gas estimates range from the US 900 trillion cubic feet to the Chinese 2 quadrillion cubic feet. Clearly China will be most interested in the exploitation of these reserves. It is also excellent reason for us to be prepared to deny the Chinese this gift of nature and exploit it ourself in concert with the countries of the South China Sea littoral. Please ask our Oil Minister to study this possibility in consultation with Chairman ONGC and revert to me in a fortnight. External Affairs Minister should be informed of our interest so that necessary tie-ups with littoral countries can be arranged. That I think, will be all for the day. Thank you both very much for your excellent briefings and advice." With these words, the Prime Minister ended the consultative meeting with the Chief of Defence Staff and the National Security Adviser.

Chapter-4

China Considers Options

Beijing, August 8, 0900 hrs

The emergency meeting of the Central Committee of the Chinese Communist Party took place at the Great Hall of the People. The meeting was chaired by Prime Minister Lung and attended by all ministers and party heads from all the provinces/regions. It was earlier rumoured that President Hong may address the meeting at some stage. Everyone in the Great Hall was eager to know what was so important about the meeting that the President himself had to come. The general view was that China may soon be at war with a neighbour—maybe South Korea or Japan or Vietnam. India had not entered anyone's mind as they believed that India was as weak as it was in 1962!

The Premier entered in style. His Cabinet colleagues greeted him outside and walked with him into the Central Hall. Everyone clapped to express their appreciation and resumed their seats. The Premier looked around and caught sight of Mr Liu who had returned a week ago from New Delhi. He nodded to Mr Liu who reciprocated.

Opening the meeting, the Premier said, "The Water Problem has become very serious. The Liu mission to New Delhi did not manage to allay Indian fears about the SNWD Project which is vital for the Country's North and North West areas where the Desert seems to be creeping in. Their reaction to our proposal was an unqualified 'No'. Our offer to give then suitable compensation for crop losses that they may suffer and a 'gift' of electricity to enable them to energise the entire 'dark' areas in India's North East, did not appeal to them. We have, therefore, to debate what we must do to tide over the water crisis and see that it doesn't occur again. I would like to ask each one of you to vote for one of three options open to us. These are: to execute the Project regardless of India's objections or, offer a further sop to India in terms of agreeing to settling the territorial disputes between them and us (except for what they call Arunachal Pradesh) more or less on their terms or, in addition, recognizing the accession in 1947 of Jammu and Kashmir to India—the last in the face of stiff opposition from our ally and friend, Pakistan. Each of these options carries a 'price tag' as it were. Going ahead without India's consent will, most probably, result in war between us and India. The settlement of the Sino-Indian border may not hold any special attraction for them unless we give up our claim on Arunachal Pradesh. And recognizing J & K as a part of India will alienate completely our ally Pakistan, who may, in concert with Afghanistan, whip up a Muslim backlash against us in Xinjiang. These are the options available. Please think over these for the next four hours including lunch in our cafeteria and reassemble here at 1400 hrs. I must ask you to be very punctual as the President will be attending the post-Lunch session from 1415 hrs onwards. Thank you."

Great Hall of the People, 1400 hrs

The Party members reassembled as required. There was a hum of conversation among them. Despite the fairly good lunch, their mood was sombre. War appeared to be the only option—a war few believed China could win in view of India having taken great strides forward in achieving a significant level of conventional military superiority over them, though not in the size of their nuclear arsenal. And none of them could even talk of nuclear war without shuddering. So it was that when President Hong (Some sycophants called him the 'Helmsman' a la Mao Zedong) entered, he found a gloomy audience waiting for him, some of them desperately fighting off post-lunch somnolence. President Hong greeted them genially, "Well, Comrades, have you considered the options the Premier had spelt out to you in the morning? Or do you need some more time to consider the problem?"

No one spoke. The question seemed to be designed only to get everyone's attention.

The President continued, "I have an additional course of action to offer for your consideration. The offer is that we seek the help of the United Nations to guarantee to us that India will not obstruct our plans as the Upper Riparian country, to exercise our sovereign right to do what we wish to with our river—the Yarlung Tsangpo. Should India decide to obstruct us, world peace will be shattered as the two most populous countries in the world would be locked in a life and death struggle for water—water from a river over which international law gives us total control. So, think again for half an hour before I ask you to vote." Immediately a buzz of conversation broke out in the Great Hall as the members discussed what the 'Helmsman' had suggested. And the President sat back in his plush throne-like chair—smiling happily at the thought that he had surely captured the House's attention.

1450 hrs

The Premier bowed to the President and banged the table with a gavel. The members fell silent almost instantly. The President then stood up and asked, "Should we try diplomacy again, but this time through the UN? And should we also use the power the Riparian law gives us over international rivers originating in our country, i.e. in Tibet? Those who wish to try what I have just explained to you, please raise your right hand." A sea of hands rose in response—it was difficult to find out if anyone had NOT raised his hand. The President, clearly aware of this difficulty, said, "Those who do NOT agree that we should give diplomacy through the UN a chance to enable us to exercise our right over the Yarlung Tsangpo, please raise your hands." Not a single hand rose. The President had got his Party's okay to move the UN in the matter and use the law to secure for them their Rights as the Upper Riparian country.

The President again addressed the House. He said, "Do not count your chickens till the eggs are hatched—is that not what your grandmother used to say? Mine did and I am, therefore, stringing a second string to our bow—this second string being further negotiations with India and

Bangladesh. I believe that they will drive a hard bargain and exact many concessions from us like recognizing their right to the whole of J & K and our full recognition of the McMahon Line—including our claim over Arunachal Pradesh. It is better that we exhaust this last option too and if all fails then we shall call upon the PLA to deliver. I am aware that India has achieved parity—maybe more than parity—with us in military capabilities; so I would like to get a couple of months more of preparation for PLA to close the gap with India. If despite all our efforts, war is thrust on us, we shall fight and WE SHALL WIN..."

And almost as if on cue the House erupted "WE SHALL WIN" endlessly for a few minutes. Everyone seemed to be on an adrenaline overdrive—such was the 'Helmsman's' magic over the House.

After a cup of tea on the lawn in the inner courtyard, the President left for his residence. Before going he asked the Premier to brief the Foreign Minister, Defence Minister, Finance Minister, Minister for Water Resources and, with their inputs and in consultation with the Chief of Judiciary, to draft their referral to the UNO. He said, "Lung, time is running out for us; the longer we delay the SNWD Project, the greater will be the desertification of our North West. If the UN gives us our right, well and good. If not, I am opting for a Sino-Indian War by end September. So get the drafts etc ready and meet me at my Residence at 1000 hrs August 10. Tsai Chien!"

President's Residence, August 10, 1000 hrs

President Hong greeted the Premier, Defence Minister, Finance Minister, Minister for Water Resources and the Chief Justice cheerfully "Before I study the Draft reference to the UNO, I would like to be clear about our legal status in the matter of the SNWD Project. Is the law in our favour, Mr Wen Leefang?"

The Chief Justice thus addressed replied, "Law on the use of river waters is based on the 'Helsinki Rules, 1966' and the United Nations Convention on the Non-Navigational Uses of International Water Courses, 1997. In the absence of a formally 'codified' and ratified international water law, customary law is what till now has to be regarded as Water Law. The Helsinki Rules and the Convention embody many of the principles of customary law and though not 'formally' law, are treated as law for all purposes. The principle underpinning riparian rights is the 'doctrine of prior appropriation'. By this, he who uses a river's water for a certain purpose is legally entitled to that right. The Upper Riparian state has first right over trans-national rivers and since China has been using the Yarlung Tsangpo waters for a long time and is also recognised as the country in which Tibet is a province or region, our use of the river in any manner we like is legal as long as we are 'reasonable' about it. The term 'reasonable' has not been defined in any of the laws quoted. Unless one regards the diversion of a river to save a large area of a highly populated country from being turned into a desert as unreasonable, I feel SNWD Project is legally sustainable."

> "Oh! You mean 'yes'—am I right?" the President asked. Taken aback, Mr Wen said, "Yes Sir. But if there are still some issues needing clarification, I can continue."

Hastily the President said, "No! No! Thank you very much Mr Wen."

The Defence Minister general Zhao Jianjing was addressed next. Asked to state how long he would take to mobilise the PLA—all three wings and the Second Artillery, he said, "All 18 combined corps of PLA maintain a high degree of operational readiness at all times. However, if a major war, i.e. offensive or defensive—is contemplated PLA as such will be fully operational in 4 weeks, this period is to recall personnel, make up shortages of equipment, ammunition and warlike stores. For calling up reservists and giving them refresher training a total of six weeks will be required."

The President asked, "Is it not a long period, 4 weeks and 6 weeks? If an aggressor attacks us, will he not run through our forward positions and be well into China by the time the combined corps are ready?"

The Defence Minister replied, "We have Border Guarding Units which are always battle ready. They cannot be brushed aside easily. The only enemy land force capable of attacking us is the Indian Army. They can be held on the border itself till the combined corps arrive on the scene—and that will be within 3-4 days as the Indian Army's movements are under constant watch and we will get early warning of their intended objectives."

"That is reassuring. What about the PLA Navy and Air Force?" asked the President.

> "PLAN and PLAAF are fully battle ready in 7 days for full scale effectiveness, about 3 days for 75 percent effectiveness and at any given time are at 25 percent effectiveness. PLAAF is undergoing extensive modernisation in relation to improving strategic early warning capability, command and control networks and for deterrent-long distance strikes. Also being developed is an Airborne Corps for developing strategic long distance strike capability. All in all, both PLAN and PLAAF are in a very satisfactory state of readiness," said the Defence Minister. Continuing, he added, "The Second Artillery Force PLASAF is instantly geared to receive a first strike and effectively retaliate within 24 hours. If we decide to carry out the first strike ourself, we are ready within 6 hours of being ordered."

"This is a healthy state for the Chinese Armed Forces,"

said the President. "As you are aware, we are distressed for fresh water in our North and North West. The Yellow River (Huang Ho) is badly polluted. We need infusion of fresh water into the North and North West of China to keep the creeping desert out and our people 'in'. To do this, we have decided to turn our river Yarlung Tsangpo, which currently flows South into India, to flow North by a gigantic engineering project—the SNWD Project. It is prohibitively expensive in terms of manpower, explosives including nuclear explosives and plant and machinery. If all goes well, we shall be able to complete the project by 2050. I hope the detailed plans are ready and the plant and machinery are available. I hope too that surveys for assessing where nuclear explosives will be required and when conventional explosives will do have been done or will be done soon. I am prepared, Finance Minister Shiao, to subordinate every other project if need be to finance the SNWD Project. Please get the estimates from the Minister for Water Resources and arrange to make funds available in time and in quantity. Finally, after I finish this talk, I shall request the Premier and Chief Justice Wen to stay back so that we can finalise our representation to the UNO." The President shook hands with the Defence Minister, Finance Minister and the Minister for Water resources and thanked them for attending the meeting. The trio thereupon left the premises.

After a short break for refreshments, the President, Premier and Chief Justice assembled in the President's study for formulating their representation to the UNO. The President briefed the Premier and Chief Justice in general terms. The 'Representation' was to be addressed to the Secretary General and copies endorsed to the United Nations Economic and Social Commission for Asia and the Pacific (UNESCAP) and United Nations Environment Programme (UNEP) and to the Government of India, Ministry of Water

Resources. It should issue from our Ministry of Water Resources and signed by the Minister.

The issues that we must raise are the critical water scarcity in North West and North China, rapid expansion of Ordas and Gobi Deserts and our compulsion to seek fresh water in large quantities on a sustained basis to save from extinction the permanent population of this region amounting to nearly 50 million people. We also need additional water to recharge the aquifers in this area as well as to restore the flow of the Yellow River (Huang Ho) which has become almost stagnant due to silting and pollution and is posing a major health hazard. After detailed study of the problem, we have reached the conclusion that Yarlung Tsangpo, a major river originating in our Tibet region and flowing first East through Tibet and then Southward into India, is the only river which can partially meet our requirement. We are already in the process of tapping the waters of other Chinese rivers in order to marginally alleviate the water-distress being experienced in the affected region in the North and North West; these projects will fructify in five years or so. The only river capable of delivering the required quantum of water is Yarlung Tsangpo—a transnational river. We, as the Upper Riparian state have informed India and Bangladesh, both benefiting from the waters of Yarlung Tsangpo about our intention to divert the Yarlung Tsangpo Northwards from the 'Great Bend Area' in Tibet, a project which will be completed in 20 years or so. We have advised both the Lower Riparian countries mentioned above about the likely diminution of the water flow in the river and our willingness to compensate them for any losses they may be put to on that account.

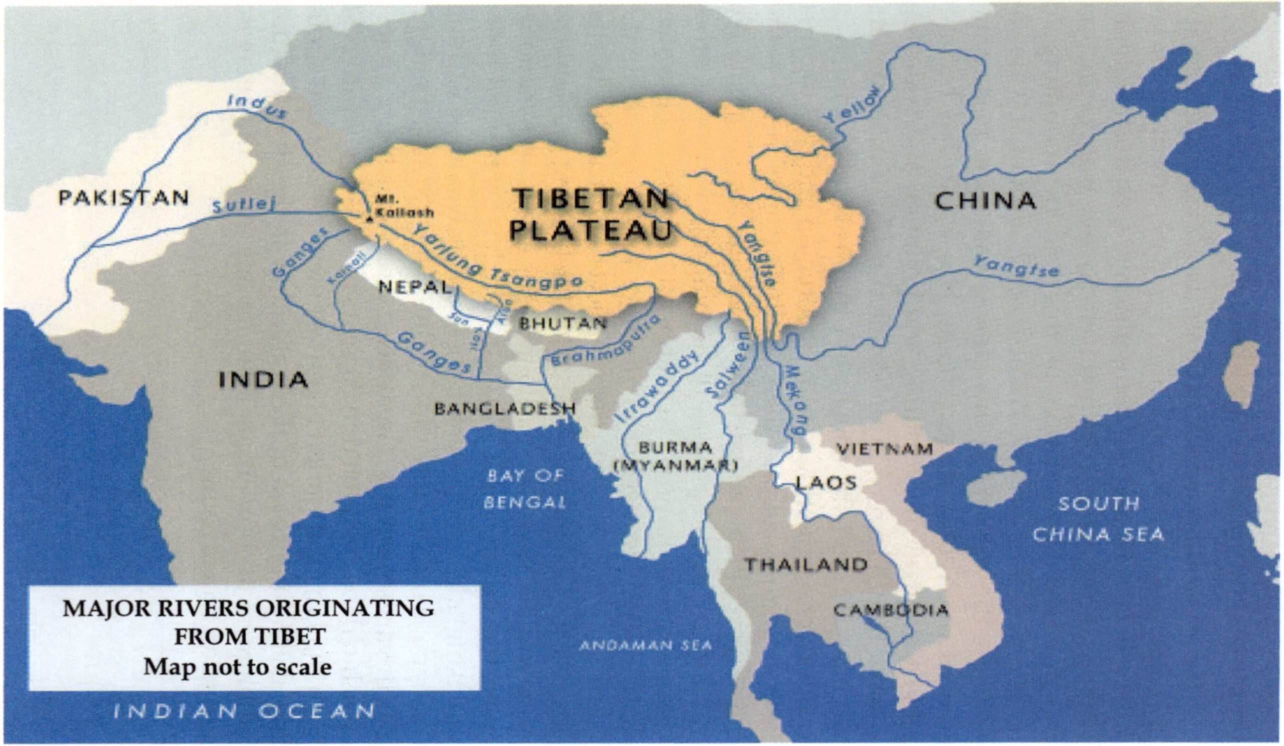

MAJOR RIVERS ORIGINATING FROM TIBET
Map not to scale

The note should conclude thus:

> "This is to inform you that as the First or Upper Riparian state, we are exercising the right vested in us to divert the waters of Yarlung Tsangpo Northwards. We request you to advise India and Bangladesh to accept our decision and our offer to compensate them for any loss to a reasonable extent."

After further discussions on the wording of the note, the President asked the Premier and Minister for Water resources to meet him again with the final draft duly cleared by the legal people on August 16. Once he approved the draft, the note must be sent by a diplomatic courier to the United Nations Headquarters in New York and delivered to concerned officials on August 17. The Premier and the Minister for Water then left the Presidential residence.

Chapter-5

Intelligence Chiefs Tasked

Beijing, August 10, 1600 hrs

Defence Minister's Office, PLA GHQ

The Heads of the Second and Third Departments, responsible for providing Military Intelligence to the PLA were ushered into the office of General Zhao Jianjing, Defence Minister, at exactly 1600 hrs. Tan Shuochi and Guo Chintao, the Heads of the Second and Third Departments, saluted General Zhao and seated themselves on the chairs indicated opposite the General.

"General Zhao got to the point without any preamble whatsoever. "We are likely to fight a war against India anytime from 15 September onwards. The reason is that India is determined not to allow us to divert the waters of Yarlung Tsangpo from South to North (our SNWD Project). Our efforts to make them agree have failed—even the offer of a handsome compensation package has been summarily turned down. President Hong has indicated that if the Indians do not agree to our demand to let our project go on without interference from them, we shall compel them to do so by waging a righteous and patriotic war against them. Since India is also a nuclear power, it is possible that they may try to deter us by threatening the use of nuclear weapons to stop our attacks against them. I shall brief you now on some points of great importance to our war effort."

"Apart from the Military Intelligence coverage that your departments provide in the normal course, in view of the political and nuclear dimensions of the forthcoming war, I would like to have specific intelligence answers to these questions:

- Is India likely to take the help of the USA or the Russian Federation—militarily or politically or by access to the latest weapons and/or intelligence sharing?
- Is Russia likely to fight against us by opening a second front from the North and North West of our country?
- What is the latest strength of India's nuclear arsenal including means of weapon delivery?
- What is the present disposition of the Indian's nuclear capable forces including submarines and naval vessels of all types? These forces must be

tagged now and their every movement must be reported to GHQ.

- What are the planned 'war locations' of India's National Command Post, HQ of Strategic Forces Command and present as well as projected locations of all 'strike' forces?
- We need accurate information of India's radar coverage over our air space as well as the Bay of Bengal—Indian Ocean—Arabian Sea areas so as to select the best areas from which to launch our missiles?
- Is India mobilizing Tibetan nationals living in India for action against us in Tibet? If so, what is their capability and strength?
- Has India entered into a mutual aid arrangement with any other country—specially Vietnam, Malaysia, Singapore, Indonesia, Myanmar and Maldives?

These are questions that you must find answers to by 1st September and with the fullest possible corroboration.

Tan and Guo enthusiastically confirmed their understanding of the task and assured the General of their ability to do so. Tan informed the General about some new Intelligence assets he had been able to create in highest echelons of the Indian Government—persons who had access to 'Top Secret' material and had been able to tap some very sensitive telephone lines—The General smiled and said, "I hope your sources will prove as good as you say without compromising their own links with us. You also need to be careful about how much you tell them as, if they are compromised, our plans may be jeopardised."

Tan assured the General on this issue. Guo, whose Department is concerned with communications security stated that his entire staff had been mobilized in view of the worsening relations with India and rigid communications security was being ensured. He had also alerted PLA Navy to ensure strict communications security was observed on all their ships and submarines as well as in foreign ports like Karachi and Hambantota where the ships may temporarily halt for any purpose. He also indicated that every message originating from the Indian Embassy or from any of its Consulates was being intercepted.

The General nodded approvingly and said, "These are difficult days for our country. So far, our neighbour India was a weak power—both politically and militarily. However, as we saw in the one day war in Pakistan held Northern Territories, they are now a force to reckon with. We need not fear them as we are stronger and wiser than them. I am sure the work of your Departments will be of great service to the cause of our Country. So, Good Luck and Thank You Comrades."

The Intelligence duo left with a spring in their steps, fully confident about their ability to fulfil the mission entrusted to them now as they had done in the past.

Chapter-6

Indians at the Golf Course

Delhi Cantonment Golf Course, August 10, 1730 hrs

The External Affairs Minister and the Defence Minister were at the seventh tee waiting for the slow moving foursome ahead to clear the fairway. But being what they are, old friends and fellow cabinet members, they decided to have a quick chat about the Chinese insistence on the

SNWD Project. Rajguru, the External Affairs Minister asked his friend Bhim Singh, the Defence Minister as to what the Chinese will do to prevent us from interfering with the work on the project. Bhim gave a quick reply, "China will tell the UNO that as they own Tibet, they have full rights to do anything they wish to with our Brahmaputra—take it north or anywhere else—even then there will be a trickle of water in the Brahmaputra basin and they will say that they have not deprived us of its water."

Rajguru reacted with a chuckle "Bhim, this is what I told the PM last night and he told me that we must displace China from owning Tibet by the simple expedient of making Tibet an independent country again. It is easier said than done, I told him. Unless the UK, USA, Europe, Russia and some others de-recognise Chinese sovereignty over Tibet, China can legally go ahead with the Project. And if we attempt to stop it by force, we shall be branded 'aggressors' and visited with world-wide sanctions against us."

Bhim said, "Our Armed Forces are capable of liberating Tibet in a short, sharp campaign lasting, maybe 15-20 days. We could clear Lhasa in about 10 days and then proclaim the Tibetan Government in Exile in Dharamsala as the legitimate Government and move it by air to Lhasa. If His Holiness gives the scheme his blessings, it will work very well."

Rajguru struck a cautious note, "The Chinese are a nuclear power with a stockpile considerably in excess of ours. If they threaten to 'nuke' value targets in North India we may find ourselves stymied. How do we overcome this problem?"

Bhim, ever the realist, replied, "He will not dare to raise his nuclear weapons against us because he knows he will get the 'bigger bang'. What is he doing this project for?—Water, isn't it? And where is the greatest store of water located? In the 'Three Gorges Dam' reservoirs. Our strategic forces, if ordered to destroy the 'Three Gorges' complex, will do so within the same day they are ordered to. Result: China will have even less water than when she started the war—probably all of the North West and North Central and West Central China will become unlivable—probably worse. No Sir, do not worry about their nukes. They are kept by them only for 'prestige' purposes!"

"I wish I could share your cheerful optimism", said Rajguru. "There is a lot of sense in what you have just said. Let us try it out on the PM after Golf."

Just then, a stentorian cry of 'Fore' from a large heavily moustachioed golfer on the fairway of the sixth forced the twosome to hastily move away. Instead of completing the game, they decided to go and meet the PM who would be at 7 RCR playing 'Scrabble' with his friend Professor Bhashyam, Head of the History Department at Jawaharlal Nehru University.

They arrived at the Gate House of 7 RCR and were quickly ushered into the Library—a medium sized book-lined room, superbly air-conditioned and lit and boasting of a king-sized Scrabble board with large pieces for the letters. Loth to disturb the great leader and the great Professor in the end stages of the ongoing game, Rajguru and Bhim made themselves comfortable with a glass each of orange juice from the sideboard and began to thumb some of the magazines lying about. Within five minutes or so, the Scrabble game was over with Professor Bhashyam having won narrowly on points. "So what brings my two major ministers here at this time?" asked the PM and before they replied, the Professor offered to leave. The PM, however, asked him to stay as they would be "talking history mainly."

The PM introduced the two ministers to the Professor. After some small talk the PM asked Rajguru and Bhim about the reason for their visit.

Speaking first, Rajguru said, "Sir, you will recall our conversation of last night regarding displacing China from being the Upper or First Riparian for all rivers originating in Tibet and, therefore, their right to use the water of these rivers in any manner they liked, including turning the river to flow towards the north instead of towards the south as is the case with the Brahmaputra. I had said that apart from India, major countries like the UK in 2008 and the USA during Mr Richard Nixon's Presidency (1969-1974) had recognised China's sovereignty over Tibet. To set the clock back and divest China of her present prerogative as the Upper Riparian State it will be necessary for Tibet to become an independent country again."

Bhim, the Defence Minister said, "Our Armed Forces could liberate Tibet in a 15-20 days campaign with Lhasa being freed in the first 10 days. As soon as Lhasa is captured, we could fly in the Tibetan Government in Exile in India, proclaim it as the legitimate Government of Tibet, thus effectively stopping the Chinese in their tracks as far as the SNWD Project is concerned. We have better than parity with the Chinese in terms of conventional warfare and the Chinese will not dare to use nuclear weapons against us since we need just one or two nuclear bombs to destroy the Three Gorges Dam and Reservoirs—a crippling blow which the Chinese will take decades to recover from, if they do recover at all."

"Very interesting conversation my ministers seem to have had on the Golf Course," said the Prime Minister to Professor Bhashyam. "Can you find a historical parallel to what Bhim has just spelt out?"

Professor Bhashyam said, "Something similar happened in 1971 in erstwhile East Bengal. You may recall that Sheikh Mujibur Rehman's Awami Party won by a huge majority in the Pakistani General Election, 1971. He had every right to expect that he would be asked to form the next Government of Pakistan. However, the non-Bengal political parties of Pakistan prevailed upon their President to deny the Sheikh this privilege he had won and to 'invite' him to Islamabad for discussions. In the event, he was arrested on arrival and a ruthless pogrom was unleashed in East Bengal. Over 10 million Bengalis fled to India from the ongoing terror campaign. Countless people were killed and women most cruelly assaulted. India helped the refugees to survive and helped their youth who formed the Mukti Fauj to carry out across the border raids against Pak occupied East Bengal. Incensed at this and alarmed by the buildup of the Indian Army for an attack on East Bengal, The Pakistani President ordered pre-emptive air strikes on all Indian Air Force bases within range. The then Prime Minister, Mrs. Indira Gandhi, in a late night broadcast over All India Radio, then announced that India had accorded political recognition to Bangladesh and that India was Bangladesh's ally in the latter's struggle against the oppressions from Pakistan. Well' that is the closest parallel to the Tibet case that I can think of though the period for which Tibet has been subjugated by China has been over 75 years.

There is, however, no question about the parallels between Bangladesh's nightmare and Tibet's longer nightmare—pogroms, genocide, rape, arson, despoiling the Tibetans of their land and what little they possessed, cultural and religious subjugation, constant attacks on priests leading to hundreds of cases of self-immolation—well, if ever there was a fit case of a country being chastised by the Free World for its crimes, China has earned that 'privilege' by her ruthless actions in Tibet. If what I have stated can be conveyed by our leaders and diplomats to the major capitals of the world and a lobby successfully created for the Independence of Tibet, then you may recognize Tibet as the Upper Riparian state and make it illegal for China to undertake the project.

My advice, therefore, is this: create a 'Free Tibet' lobby in London, Washington, Berlin, Moscow, Paris and some other countries as soon as you can; while this process is going on, organize Tibetan fighters to carry out repeated raids on Chinese installations and facilities in that country so as to make Chinese counter action more reprehensible to the Free World; then recognise Tibet as a free country with His Holiness as the Spiritual-cum-Temporal Head of State and the Tibetan Government in Exile as the Interim Government of the 'Republic of Tibet'. Launch operations soon after this to capture Lhasa and major towns and habitations along the Karakoram and Xinjiang Highways ensuring all the while that Chinese Prisoners of War are treated humanely and repatriated only when every form of anti-Tibet action by PRC is ended. I am no politician nor am I a soldier. However, given the decades of slavery Tibet has suffered and the atrocities it has been a victim of, I think this is the least we can do for the brave Tibetan people."

"What a wonderful talk you have given, Bash. I am deeply indebted to you. When the hurly-burly is over and done with, I shall invite you to accept the honorary rank of a Major General in the Indian Army. Please do not turn it down when the time comes. Thank you once again, my friend. Gentlemen, kindly see off the Professor and meet me tomorrow along with the National Security Advisor at 0900 hrs in my South Block Office."

As they changed cars at the security post near the gate, Rajguru and Bhim were effusive in praising the Professor for his admirable advice. The Professor for his part said, "I think both of you were thinking almost exactly what I got the opportunity to articulate. Thank you, Gentlemen." The cars moved off and merged with the general traffic on Race Course Road.

Chapter-7

Incidents and Reactions

Dingri, Tibet

August 10, Noon

The Chomolungma (Mt Everest) Massif cast a huge shadow over Dingri area, an insignificant hamlet on the northern side of Everest. A track once surfaced with compacted rubble and now a mere trace on the icy surface, lay five kilometres to the east. The track ran from the Chinese Task Force camp, further North, to the Hydel Project area at

Qudang. It was used twice a month for carrying out relief of the workers at the Project site by a fresh batch from the camp and replenishment of supplies.

Two half tracked military vehicles of two tonnes capacity each, moved slowly towards Qudang, 30 minutes driving time away. 20 fresh workers with supplies for three weeks and some project stores were being carried by this small convoy. Except for the drivers and one or two others, the relief party was asleep.

Karma Tenzin grinned at his party of six personnel from the Khampa Scouts. The sleeping persons in the Chinese convoy were due to have a noisy awakening in about five minutes, when they reached the mines laid by the Scouts on the track.

Karma triggered the firing switch at 1204 hrs. The two trucks were blown to bits, some parts of these flying as high as 30 metres. With their weapons ready to fire if need be, the Scouts approached the ambush site with great care. They did a quick check for survivors. Except for three persons who were still alive but unconscious, there was no survivor. The three still living were shot in the head and killed. The party stripped the trucks of whatever they found useful. Four Chinese made automatics, two short range walkie-talkies and a sack containing tinned food stuffs were loaded on their two sledges. They left the scene of the ambush after smashing the convoy's long range wireless set, at 1215 hrs on skis, towing their loaded sledges and made their way to their hide some 10 kilometres away.

The Site Engineer at Qudang realised that something had happened to the relievers when they did not reach even by 1500 hrs; nor did they answer any call on the wireless. In any case, he was not in a position to physically send a party to trace the convoy as his own transport was non-functional. At 1600 hrs, he radioed the depressing news of the missing convoy to the Task Force Camp.

A blizzard sprang up around 1600 hrs and blotted out most of the debris and bodies at the ambush site. An up-ended axle, which somehow got embedded into the track in that position mutely told the story of the Dingri ambush to the patrol that reached the site 24 hours later. It was the second ambush of Chinese vehicles in the last 10 days in Tibet.

The Chinese Reaction, August 11 onwards

The ambush alarmed the Chinese. Orders were issued to provide PLA escorts to all vehicle convoys. Single vehicles were not to ply in future. Movement could take place only after the route of movement was gone over by a 'road opening' party, which deployed three-man picquets at suitable places after 'opening' the road. Movement, therefore, became slower and expensive in terms of troops used. These orders were made applicable to all of Tibet, where, due to frequent sniping at Chinese personnel/ vehicles, the mood was already sombre. Morale, both civilian and military hit a new low. The Chinese Government in Tibet was rather worried and decided to take steps to restore morale.

The route the Chinese took to restore morale would have found approval from the late Adolf Hitler and his minions in Nazi Germany. It was the route of reprisal, thuggery and mass killing. Unconsciously they exhibited their fear by their systematic brutality. This was duly noted by German and British tourists who had come to Tibet to study Buddhism and how it was different in Tibet in its form, observances and theology from what is prevalent in the land of its birth—India. They cut short their study tour and flew out to New Delhi where, before a shocked worldwide TV audience, they showed what they saw of the face of PRC in Occupied Tibet. The civilized world was appalled and revolted by the Chinese actions and, when despite being put on cautionary notice the Chinese did not mend their ways, imposed economic sanctions against China.

China stepped up its repression of Tibetans. Raids like the 'catch and kill' raids practiced by the Gestapo during World War II became the vogue. Numerous 'out of hand' executions were reported from Lhasa, Shigatse, Gyangze, Amdo and many other places. These activities were carried out in defiance of World opinion and cost the Chinese dear.

The ever increasing Chinese brutality towards Tibetans saddened His Holiness, the Dalai Lama. He, who is regarded as God-incarnate said in a public message carried live by almost every TV channel in the world, "The road to Freedom is hard and flush with horrors; and yet, we must walk the distance in order to preserve our Nationhood and Buddhist culture." It was virtually a clarion call for a general uprising in Tibet.

The Chinese adopted yet another plan to discipline the Tibetans—control of food. All over Tibet, as on a cue, simultaneous raids were carried out to confiscate stocks of rice, corn, wheat, spices of various types and so on. This measure began to have effect after a week or so. The Tibetans retaliated by ambushing supply convoys and on two occasions raiding the Chinese Supply Depots at Yatung and Gartok. These raids were overshadowed by increased sabotage activities directed at the oil pipelines from Gormo to Lhasa and fuel depot at Shigatse. It was clear to the Chinese that the Tibetans had not been subdued by any of the methods they had adopted so far. It seemed very likely that they were being helped by a neighbour—India. They decided to work out their frustration on the India-Tibet border.

They first turned their eyes towards the Sikkim border where they had tried something similar about 50 years ago at Nathula and came off with a large number of their personnel being killed or wounded. From August 15 to August 16, Indian Army positions at Nathula and another pass on the Watershed, Jelepla, were shelled heavily at intervals by long range guns and mortars. Indian troops, well protected by their concrete bunkers waited for the Indian Artillery's response which came only on August 17. And what a response it was too! A battery of Indian made multi-barrelled rocket launchers opened retaliatory fire for a few minutes. The Battery fired two salvoes and delivered a crippling 96 rockets with thermo-baric warheads with pinpoint accuracy at a range of 40 kms—out of the Chinese Artillery range. The first battery was silenced and took no further part in the proceedings. A similar retaliatory attack was carried out on the Second Chinese battery with similar results. The Indian Rocket batteries had been held up by a huge landslide when they were moving from Siliguri to Sikkim—hence the delayed but, nevertheless, deadly response. As one soldier at Nathula put it *'Der aye lekin durust aye'* (Late in coming but 'Bang on' on target).

By this time, the news of hostilities between China and India in the Sikkim-Yatung Sector had reached the world capitals. USA, UK, USSR, France, Germany, Japan and Vietnam warned the Chinese to stop provocative actions on the Tibet-India border. The US, UK and France also roundly condemned the Chinese atrocities against the Tibetan people and warned China that any further atrocities in Tibet or border fringes against India, will invite joint action by these major powers and severe strictures from the UN Security Council. This reaction on the part of the major powers forced China to stop their anti-Tibetan actions and border firing against Indian posts—at least for the present.

Off the Coast of Vietnam: August 19

In a rather strange manner, India and China confronted each other in South China Sea. A flotilla of Indian Navy consisting of one Destroyer and three frigates was on a good-will visit to Vietnam. When the Vietnamese coast was still some 12 nautical miles distant, a PLA Navy Frigate along with maritime patrol vessels challenged the Indian flotilla and demanded that they leave South China Sea immediately as these are Chinese waters and the IN flotilla had entered without prior permission! The Indian Commodore on board the Destroyer had this message sent to the Chinese:

> "These are international waters. Go back where you came from or face the consequences."

The Chinese Frigate and patrol boats moved very quickly away towards Hainan from where they had come.

Vietnam sent a protest note to the Chinese observing that such unilateral assumption of international waters being their territory is baseless, illogical and condemnable. They demanded that the Chinese desist from any such high handed action in future.

Chapter-8

Some Intelligence Reports

Beijing, August 10, 2359 hrs

Second Department—TIBINT Room

Tan Shuochi was studying the cipher message that had been sent by his agent in Bhaktapur, Central Nepal. The Agent, Wang Renwei had been 'seeded' into Central Nepal some years ago to keep an eye on Tibetan training activities in high altitude areas of Central and Western Nepal. To the Nepalis, he had the impeccable cover of a vagabond drink addict who lived off what he could get from mountaineering expeditions for work done for them and by joining various parties—some Indian, some Tibetan and some Japanese who would periodically land up in Bhaktapur to train for their expedition to one of the Himalayan peaks. To the man's immense credit, it must be said that he looked more like a Nepali or Indian and certainly not like a Chinese or Tibetan. It was his deciphered report that had caused Tan to rush to the TIBINT room. This is what the brief message read:

Most Secret

Flash

From: Agent Hsia **Dto: 09 2300 Hrs**

For: Gen Tan Shuochi, Second Department (.) Information (.) A party of Tibetan hostiles left on 06 Aug via difficult mountaineering route for general area Qudang (.) strength of party 1 Ldr and 6 OR (.) party carrying personal small arms, explosives and two mines, possibly antitank (.) mission clearly is sabotage (.) target may be Qudang Hydel Project or disruption of traffic on East-West Highway (.) message ends Tan Shuochi was pleased at his agent's performance. So far, nothing had happened in the likely target area. He decided to send a general alert to Qudang Hydel Project and to checkpoints along the Highway. Unfortunately a blizzard was ranging North of the Mount Everest Massif and radio communications were not restored till dawn on August 11.

Beijing, August 12, 1200 hrs

Most Secret

Flash

From: Agent Huang **DTO: 11 1800 hrs**

For: Gen Tan Shuochi, Second Department (.) Information (.) a military special train has arrived at New Jalpaiguri and all other traffic on the railway route has been frozen till the train is moved to New Mal station (.) train being heavily guarded by army personnel(.) discreet stand off observation suggests approximately 12 large sized vehicles with some large caliber weapons fitted to the vehicles (.) infer heavy long range guns or multi barrelled rocket launchers (.) weapons likely to be inducted into Sikkim Sector (.) am moving now towards upper Teesta river bridge with necessary stores to set off a large land slide on Road Siliguri-Gangtok with my colleague in our Jeep (.) message ends

Gen Tan Shuochi was happy to read Agent Huang's report. The large landslide would be welcome to the forces ordered to retaliate by artillery fire against the Indians for their equipping and assisting the ambush party at Dingri. The Indian retaliation to the Chinese fire assaults will certainly be affected. "Well Done Agent Huang" Tan murmured to himself.

Chapter-9

Rebels Around China

Urumqi, Xinjiang

August 19

Intercept from the clandestine 'Uyghur Freedom Radio' operating from somewhere around Urumqi, the provincial capital is reproduced below:

"A shoot out took place in Kashgar between Uyghur freedom fighters and Tungan traitors serving the

Chinese. The incident was caused by the Tungans attempting to seize the house and shop of Yunus Mohammad, 52 years old. The Tungans forcibly entered Yunus' shop in which two friends of Yunus—Maqsud Khan and Musa Kadir, who, armed as usual, were waiting. They fired on the Tungans. The Tungans were five in all. All of them were killed by the brave Uyghurs, who, along with their families have escaped to safer places. Request to listeners: please pass this report verbally to other Uyghurs."

Overheard in the market of Urumqui, the following points are of interest:

- The main Tungan killed in the shootout has been identified as Yakub, son of late Tungan General Bai Chong Shi.
- Bai Chung Shi was responsible for the present subjugation by the Chinese as he led the Division which crushed the Uyghur revolt.
- A fresh alliance between Kirghiz and Uyghur people is likely to take shape. Some Kazakhs who were press-ganged to work on Chinese construction projects are also likely to join them. If this materialises, the Uyghurs will be able to harass the Chinese so much that either they will leave them and go back to China or, deploy large number of troops against them. Either way, the weak would have frightened the strong!

Uyghur Freedom Radio broadcast the following warning:

- The Tungans are thirsty for revenge. Yunus' vacant house and shop have been ransacked by Tungans and later burnt down. Tungans are warned that this atrocity will be punished in due course.

- All patriotic Uyghurs are advised to take no Tungan or Chinese at face value. They are poison.

Erenhot, Inner Mongolia

August 20, Dawn

Gansukh and his five friends proceeded cautiously as they neared the border with the Republic of Mongolia. Thanks to the extremely cold winds that can freeze one's blood as it were, the Chinese never patrolled the border at dawn. And that is why Gansukh and party had chosen to cross over to the Republic of Mongolia at that time.

At the pre-arranged rendezvous, their Mongolian guide was waiting for them. He had the papers that would enable them to move to the airport at Ulanbator, the Capital. Their flights to New Delhi and thence to Srinagar had also been arranged along with the necessary documents. Everything worked as planned and after a while, they were in the aircraft flying to India—fast asleep.

Srinagar was very pleasant as was Gulmarg where they were to be put through a three weeks course on high altitude warfare followed by a week long course on explosives, mines and other such devices.

Gansukh could speak English and was able to ensure that his friends too followed what was being taught to them by their trainers. He and his group amazed their instructors by their intelligence and grasp, stamina in the mountains and ability to do with very little sleep or rest.

By mid September, they were on their way back to Ulanbator and thence to the Chinese province of Nei Monggol. Gansukh vowed that Nei Monggol would be freed from the Han Chinese within this year. It was going to be hard work but they were confident and ready.

Sogo Nur, Inner Mongolia

September 19, Midnight

Gansukh had noted with dismay that their post-1998 settlement had been 'invaded' by two busloads of Han settlers. He was quite sure that the meagre resources of water, pasturage and shelter could not support the additional 50 people who had landed up in their settlement—not for long. He was determined that the settlers must go, one way or another. He had shared this view with their settlement 'Elder', Nergui earlier on in the evening. Nergui said that he would think it over and asked him to come back in one hour for a decision.

It was a terrible decision Nergui had to make. He and his people at Sogo Nur were themselves ousted from their original homeland in Wuhai area, some 600 kilometres to the east. And now here are 50 more people of a different stock—the more aggressive Han stock—who had come into Sogo Nur. He asked himself whether they would have to become 'oustees' again. He shook his head vehemently. When Gansukh came in again, he nodded assent. He said to him, "Be kind. Give them a swift and smooth departure from this world." Gansukh nodded and with his India returned 'course mates' set about preparing the explosive charges to blow up everything in their five tents. They had enough explosives with them for many such missions as the generous Indians had given them four suitcases filled with a variety of explosives, the suitcases being innocuously described as personal effects and pushed through Customs both in India and at Ulanbator.

By midnight the preparations were completed. Gansukh and party laid their explosives at the scale of two to a tent—one forward and another aft—so that the Claymore mine type devices would pepper everyone with high velocity missiles—ball bearings, nails and lethal gas canisters that would release their contents after a ten second delay after the main explosion.

At midnight, precisely, the deed was done. 50 Han settlers at Sogo Nur had been killed in their sleep. The entire settlement turned out to remove the human and material debris to a point some 500 metres distant where there was a dry salt-water pond which had dried up years ago. By daybreak all trace of the late Hans had been effaced while a strong westerly wind concealed the tracks made by the two buses as well as all traces of the explosions and the subsequent burial.

No one in China came to know anything about the Sogo Nur incident—and probably, they had greater problems to contend with than worry about 50 people having disappeared off the face of the Earth.

Urumqi, Xinjiang

August 25

The Uyghurs were determined to punish the Chinese imperialists and their lackeys, the Tungans for the destruction of Yunus' house and property following the killing of Yakub and four other Tungans on August 12. They decided to concentrate their attention on Han Chinese patrols and Police personnel. To get them into the trap, a large anti-Chinese rally was organised on August 17 with information about the time and place being deliberately passed on to the Chinese. It worked as they planned it. The 1200 strong rally was confronted by two companies of China (Han) Police from three different directions. There were approximately 180 Chinese policemen in all and each of the three groups was about 60 strong. As they sought to arrest the rallyists, they were attacked by armed Uyghurs hiding in houses on either side of the main road and lanes leading up to it. One group was almost entirely wiped out—50 policemen having been killed. The other two groups, in the face of withering small arms and machine gun fire, both firing too high to kill anyone close enough to do so any time, offered to surrender. They dropped their arms on the road and sheep-like huddled together under the menacing machine guns of the Uyghurs.

On the captured Police radio, the Uyghur Chief sent a message to Police HQ, Xinjiang for immediate passage to Beijing. The message read as follows;

> "You had sent two companies of Police to chastise us when we were holding a peaceful rally. Your Han soldiers fired on unarmed, peaceful rallyists and killed and wounded some of them. We had anticipated such inhuman behaviour from you and had held a number of armed men of the Uyghur National Army on side lanes leading to the rally site. They swung into counter action and in the process, 50 of your men have been killed. We have in our custody nearly 120 more of your men and so far, we have done no more than slap them around. All of them are safe. If you wish to see them back again, you will, first of all recognise, so that the world will know, our freedom under the name 'The Islamic Republic of East Turkestan'. You will then order out of Xinjiang which is our land, all Chinese of Han stock. You may also take away the despicable Tungan if you like to have traitors with you. Once you have complied with these two conditions—i.e. Free Us and Get Out—we shall decide about releasing the Han prisoners we hold. If our conditions are not met within 24 hours, their lives will be forfeited. If you accept and comply with our demands, we shall release them unharmed."

There was consternation in Beijing and, as they say in a certain genre of books 'much wailing and gnashing of teeth'. But the Chinese knew that they had to agree. They did this as gracelessly as they could in a radio message which read as under:

> "The People's Republic of China has been coerced by Uyghur bandits holding 120 Chinese Police personnel hostage to recognise the independence of Xinjiang under the label 'Islamic Republic of East Turkestan'. We reject this part of their demand as it is absurd and demeaning. However, we agree to carry out full evacuation of all Chinese living in Xinjiang to neighbouring states. We demand that the Uyghurs forthwith release the hostages held by them or face the full might of the People's Republic of China."

Surprisingly, the Uyghurs were quite satisfied with the partial acceptance of their conditions and they watched the exodus of the Chinese in trucks, buses and cars on the Xinjiang Highway towards Pusa, 85 km away. In glee over their easy victory, they fired towards the general direction of the evacuees without hitting any vehicle or person—a juvenile but harmless display of sheer animal spirits.

The matter was not over as the hostages were still in Uyghur custody. In response to a question from a BBC reporter, the Uyghur Chief Justice of the Special Sharia Court Muhammad Maqsud Jenghiz stated, "The Special Sharia Court has just now been constituted. Those persons who had fired at the peaceful demonstrators and killed many of them will be tried under Islamic Law."

When pressed to state what punishments the Court could award, he said, "For causing death, the death penalty; for causing injuries, similar but more severe injuries will be suffered by the guilty." The media in the entire Middle-East, Pakistan, Afghanistan and Indonesia hailed this reply as 'fair'. Media in Bangladesh, India and most western countries advised moderation! An Indian politician, known for his uninhibited comments said, "So far they trampled on the Uyghurs; now it is the turn of the Chinese to be trampled." The worm had, indeed, turned.

Chapter-10

Intelligence Summary: August 2029

Secret

Compiler: Director Dai Ziping

Station: New Delhi, India

1. **General**

   The abrupt breakdown of talks between our delegation and those of India and Bangladesh, has been widely commented upon by all news papers in this country. The stilted manner of reporting on the event clearly indicates anti-China sentiment and efforts to portray China as attempting to steal India's water. One Hindi newspaper 'Kranthi' editorially threatened war against China if any attempt is made to divert Brahmaputra River.

2. **Meeting/Conference**

   A meeting was held in 7 Race Course Road, residence of the Indian Prime Minster, to consider the outcome of the failed talks between China and India—Bangladesh on 1st August. Our informant who monitored the listening device planted in a flower vase kept on the conference table, stated that India means to stop the SNWD Project at any cost and to deprive China of its right to undertake this project as the source-country of Yarlung Tsangpo and will make all-out efforts to make Tibet an independent country again. The listening device did not transmit any further for reasons unknown.

3. India's Permanent Representative at the UN met the Indian Prime Minister on 3rd August. He was later closeted with the Indian Law Minister and left after two hours of discussion with him for his hostel accommodation. He was carrying books given to him by the Law Minister—presumably on law relating to rights over river waters. India's Permanent Representative at the UN met the Indian Prime Minister on 3rd August.

4. The Prime Minister held a meeting in his office on 8th August with the National Security Advisor and Chief of Defence Staff. Our sources in the PM's office said that place names such as Xinjiang, Kazakhstan, Nei Monggol and Tibet were frequently mentioned. There was also some discussion on visits by Indian Navy ships to Vietnam, Philippines, Brunei and

Malaysia. It is inferred that India may be planning to create problems for us in Xinjiang and Nei Monggol and establishing closer relations with South East Asian countries in view of our domination of the South China Sea.

5. **Social Events**

Professor Bhashyam, Head of the History Department at Jawaharlal Nehru University visited the Prime Minister at his residence for a game of Scrabble—a routine event.

6. The two were later joined by the External Affairs Minister and Defence Minister. They were all together for one hour. The Professor and the two Ministers left the PM's Residence together. It is likely that they discussed the SNWD project in the light of historical parallels and possibly military action to stop the project.

7. **Border Incident**

From 15th to 17th August, Chinese guns and rocket launchers shelled Indian forward positions in Sikkim's Nathu La and Jelep La areas. There were only six Indian casualties—two soldiers killed at Nathu La and two civilians wounded at Sherathang. No casualty was reported on the Jelep La side.

8. Indian retaliation took place on 17th August. Indian long range, multi-barrelled rocket batteries with a total of 12 launchers fired 96 rockets each against Chinese guns opposite Nathu La and Jelep La. It is noteworthy that the Indian launchers were 35-40 kms from the Sikkim Watershed. After they fired no further firing took place.

9. **Naval Encounter**

Naval Headquarters, New Delhi was abuzz with

conversation among Naval officers about an encounter between an Indian Navy flotilla and a PLA Navy Frigate and maritime patrol crafts off the coast of Vietnam. The PLAN Frigate challenged the Indian flotilla for their presence in Chinese waters. Indians threatened grave consequence if the Chinese party did not withdraw immediately. This, the Chinese party did.

10. Conclusion

The SNWD Project appears to have become a major issue on which the Indian point of view is directly opposite that of our Country. It seems likely to develop further into a major flash point between our countries in the next four to six weeks or so. Ad interim Indians are likely to take recourse to creating trouble for us in Xinjiang and Nei Monggol. They are also likely to step up Naval activities in the South China Sea and seas/ocean girdling India.

11. Our country should be prepared for war within four to six weeks.

New Delhi	Sd/Dai Ziping
31st August 2029	Station Director

Chapter-11

China Sees Red

President's Residence, Beijing

September 21, 1000 hrs

President Hong was livid with anger when he heard the details of the Urumqi incident. Coming as it did soon after an unexplained fire in the Sogo Nur border region of Nei Monggol—a chance pick up by a low orbiting Chinese satellite transiting 200 km above the Earth on the 19th. It could not be explained by anyone. A helicopter sortie sent over that area where the satellite imagery had shown a fire, returned with a completely normal report. The pilot had photographed the Sogo Nur settlement where the fire had been detected by satellite imagery. The photograph showed a normal tented/hutted settlement where nothing unusual could be detected. In fact, the pilot reported that an elderly man and a small boy came out of their tent and waved to the helicopter pilot. The small boy also gave a cracking good salute! Mr Hong was still wondering about the fire picked up by the satellite on the night of September 19. At this time, his Aide announced the arrival of the Prime Minister Mr Lung. The President shrugged off his worry about the satellite imagery and went to his study to which the Aide had taken the Premier as desired by him.

After exchange of greetings, the President shared with the Premier his anguish at what had been happening since the July 31 meeting on the SNWD Project with ministers from India and Bangladesh. The President said, "That was a very blunt rebuff that man Iyengar gave us. Our delegation had to return with 'red' faces." The President chuckled at his unintended piece of humour and continued, "Then came the Dingri Ambush with so many good men killed. What was worse was the criticism the world media gave us for our just reaction against the wretched Tibetans. Our artillery attack against the Indians was a sad experience too; the rascals kept silent for two days and then blasted us with those horrid multi-barrel rocket launchers with extra-powerful ammunition. Our fellows could not hit back at them because they were out-ranged by the Indians. This is the second time Sikkim has been unlucky for us—the last was almost 50 years ago!" He continued, "Our attempt at controlling access to the South China Sea failed miserably when the Indian flotilla chased away the coastal protection craft and the distasteful rebuke we got from Vietnam for our scrape with the Indian Navy—and these Vietnamese are supposed to be Communists too!" He took a deep breath and a cup of Chinese green tea and looked at the placid surface of the lake nearby.

"Now I come to the disgraceful incident at Urumqi. The rebel Uyghurs set up a trap for us and our Police force—180 persons—walked into it and got into a 'wei qi' sort of situation—could move neither right nor left, nor forward or backward—could only drop their weapons and meekly surrender to the rebels after taking a few casualties! And the rebels made their most insulting demand for recognition as a republic—what did they tell us—'Free us and Get out!' it rankles. Our national honour has been sullied. We need to redeem it."

The President looked hard at the Premier. He said, "Comrade Lung! Enough of this lamenting like old women. We have to get back to things we can control, tasks which we can set for ourselves and complete. And in the fullness of time, we shall move against each one of our enemies and make them regret they crossed our path. Now: what is the progress on the Water Diversion Project?"

The Premier, who was dreading this question, said, "I am happy to say that Project work in the form of survey of the alignment of the tunnels in the Bayankala Mountains Sector has been completed except that an earth tremor on the alignment we had selected and surveyed made it seem unsuitable. We are now in the process of selecting a new alignment and our seismologists, hydro-engineers and other scientists are working round the clock to establish a relatively safe alignment through the Bayankala Mountains."

"What do you mean by 'relatively safe'? Do you mean to tell me that whatever the alignment we may take, we can still be affected by the tremors? Surely, if the hydro-engineers found the first alignment most suitable for the flow of water let us go firm on that alignment and let the seismologists do their best at quake prediction and advise our engineers on shoring up the flow channel in the 300 kilometres of quake prone Bayankala."

"We shall carry out your directions immediately. I am sure we shall find a way—perhaps a system of multiple channels through the quake prone area with switching made possible from a closed channel to an unaffected channel anywhere in the Bayankala Mountains. The costs will be greater but regardless of quakes, the Yarlung Tsangpo will reach the upper reaches of the Yellow River as planned."

The President was mollified by the Premier's confidence and determination. He told him quite plainly that this is the sort of approach that will get the Project through—the search for bypassing problem areas and multiple channels for one river to flow through. "Go ahead Lung and may the 'Great Helmsman' guide you in spirit to success," said the President as he saw the Premier off at his doorstep.

The Premier left to attend a meeting with the seismologists, hydro-engineers and other scientists at Lanzou where they had a Scientists' Camp complete with a laboratory with all necessary facilities like Core Sample Analysis, Digital Seismic Monitor and so on. He would be just in time to lunch with them and have a long session with the scientists and engineers.

Camp Lanzou, 1400 hrs

The Premier had a working lunch with the Project Team. Now they turned their attention to the problem of how to convey the waters of the Yarlung Tsangpo, if and when it reaches this far, across the earthquake prone zone of the Bayankala Mountains, to the upper reaches of the Yellow River. The mood was serious and somewhat pessimistic.

The Premier recounted the salient points of his discussions with the President about the Project. The discussion next centred round the probability of occurrence of earthquakes in this region. Dr Lee, Chief Seismologist stated that major earthquakes are rare in this area as per the seismic records he has examined. The most powerful quake recorded in this region was in 1995. It measured 5.9 on the Richter scale. "From 1995 onwards," Dr Lee continues, "This region has regularly experienced tremors measuring between 3 and 4.5 on the Richter scale every two to three months. The last tremor we had here 15 days ago was recorded at 3 on the Richter scale. If the past record is any guide, we are not due for a quake of any sort for at least 45 days—and a minor one at that." Just as he said this, a deep rumbling noise seemed to rise out of the mountain's bowels as it were. Then came a few vicious cracks and the earth began to shake as though it was being pummelled by an angry giant.

It was a strong earthquake—and when he confirmed its strength from his laboratory's digital seismic monitor, he was shocked to find that it was recording 7.2 on the Richter scale—just about as bad as it can get in a mountainous region. This quake was found to have done extensive damage to the Bayankala Range; it had caused 12 major land slips, cut open a wide gash in the East-West direction—the gash going across five spurs emanating from the mountain massif, at places 10 metres wide—and toppled countless trees. And it could not have come at a worse time for the Premier and Dr Lee.

Dr Lee was too stunned to speak. The Premier, however, kept cool and tried to bring him out of the state of shock he was in. A glass of water helped him and in a few minutes Dr Lee was himself again—a bit apologetic for his optimistic prediction just before the quake—but, a top-notch seismologist once again. He told the Premier, "I am sorry about my mistake. But this sort of a surprise nature can spring on anyone at any time. If I have your approval, I shall go over the records of previous quakes here, this quake too—in detail—assess the likely effect it may have on our Project and come up with some viable solution to our problem of getting the Yarlung Tsangpo's water to the Yellow River. It may take some 10 to 15 days for all this, so please bear with me."

The premier, essentially a kind-hearted man, said, "Go ahead Dr Lee. I shall not be disturbing you for two weeks. I shall advise the President of what transpired today and of your determination to find an answer to our problem. Till then Tsai Chien." He left for his helicopter with a chorus of Tsai Chiens sounding in his wake. Though he was an agnostic, he shut his eyes as though in prayer. In fact he was praying—not to an unknown Divinity, but to the one every one in China called 'the Great Helmsman'—late Mao Zedong.

September, 21, 0900 hrs

Road Bomi-Metok Counties

The red coloured taxi turned off National Highway No 318 on to the 15 year old Road Bomi-Metok. The four occupants and driver wore the usual dress of road maintenance workers. Their equipment too bore testimony to their occupation. The Sergeant at the Traffic Check Post Zhamog waved them on their way with the advice that a slide had occurred at Km 58—at the midpoint of the road. He wished them good luck. The gang in the Red taxi thanked the Sergeant and proceeded on their mission.

Their mission had been misconstrued by the good Sergeant. Their task was not road repair but road demolition—at a number of places so as to make the road unusable for at least 10 days. They carried the necessary demolition charges into which they had simply to insert the 'time-pencil' to arm the charge. Before leaving, they had to break the time pencil and go away. When the acid completed its work, the detonator would be ignited and in a second or so, the charge would explode bringing down a large section of the road in the form of a land-slide. With four such slides at Kilometres 28, 38, 48 and 58 they reckoned that they may be able to make the road unusable for even longer than 10 days. They got to each of the selected sites, spent only five minutes in placing the charges and inserting the time pencils taking care not to break them till all the charges had been laid. When they started their return journey to Zhamog, it had taken them about nine hours in all including travel time and 20 minutes for laying the demolition charges. They also spent a final five minutes at Km 43 to pray to Goddess Dorje Phagmo for the success of their mission and to offer Her their apologies for setting off noisy explosions so close to the most sacred 'beyul' of 'Pema Koe'. Having done their task and said their prayers, the party returned to the Zhamog Check Post. The same Sergeant was still on duty and greeted them warmly. They chatted with him for a couple of minutes and requested if they could use his communication equipment to report to their base. The Sergeant informed them that the radio had been sent to the workshop at base and will not be back for a couple of days. However they could telephone their base from the Check Post. After thanking him, the leader of the group Tashi Rinchen, Commando Sergeant ex No 1 Special Forces Battalion of Free Tibet Army, shot the Check Post Sergeant through the back of his head. The Commandos then drove at a good speed to Bomi from where at night they made their way to the Tibet-India border (McMahon Line) reaching India by first light next day.

September 22, 0800 hrs

Itanagar (Capital of Arunachal Pradesh)

The morning news bulletin at 6 AM from Beijing did not mention anything unusual. However, the 8 AM bulletin was almost 'hysterical', reporting the four explosions at 10 km intervals on the road linking Bomi and Metok Counties and leading to Metok close to the Indian border. After a full minute of 'ranting' about the dastardly action yesterday by a group of Special Forces soldiers presumed to be Indians, the news reader suddenly broke off and a few seconds later flashed a news item in bold red characters reading in the English translation as "It has just been revealed that the commando operation yesterday had at least one Tibetan. At km 43 on the road that was attacked, at a point exactly midway between the first and fourth explosions, traces of a Tibetan having offered prayers were found. Recovered from the site were one prayer scarf, one joss stick partially burnt, stub of a candle and a packet of Indian sweetmeats. Top officials in Beijing stated that Indians are now using Tibetans to attack China. The Government will take up the matter with the UN Security Council."

The Chief Minister laughed uproariously. He said, "The entire road has been knocked off over a 30 km stretch. The God is kind indeed. Our Chinese friends, specially their President Hong and Premier Lung must be seeing red." He went to the adjacent room and said, "Well done and au revoir" to Commandos Tashi Rinchen, Lobsang Norbu, Jigme Phuntsok, Dolma Topdin and Sonam Dorjee. The beaming Tibetan Commander's departure from Itanagar helipad was shown all over the world on TV including China. They all saw Red.

Chapter-12

At the United Nations

UN Headquarters, New York

Security Council Chamber, September 22, 1000 hrs

Secretary General Mr Robert Starr confirmed from the members that they have received and read the President of the People's Republic of China's reference on the Water Dispute. He then called upon Mr Dmitri Pavlov of Russia to assume the President's chair and conduct the proceedings.

"This Special Meeting has been called in order to consider the Representation made to the UN by the People's Republic of China (PRC) regarding their rights as the Upper Riparian in respect of all rivers originating in Tibet Region of China, more specifically on the river Yarlung Tsangpo or Brahmaputra as it is known in India. This Representation arises out of the fact that PRC wants to divert the main course of the river from flowing south into India and engineer it to flow northwards toward North West/North China. As the Upper Riparian Country PRC was obliged to consult neighbours India and Bangladesh as the diversion of the river northwards will reduce the availability of fresh water to India by over 30 per cent and Bangladesh even more. The tripartite meeting took place at New Delhi on July 31, 2029. PRC accepted that there will be some loss of water inflow to these two countries with consequent adverse effects on agriculture, ecology including both flora and fauna, river navigability, shrinking of the Delta of the river Meghna/ Jumna (the names used in Bangladesh for the Brahmaputra and a gradual infiltration of sea water into the relatively dry beds of these rivers. PRC offered to compensate the two countries for notional crop loss and ecological damage. However, both India and Bangladesh have flatly turned down the PRC proposal and expressed strong objection to any tampering with the flow of the Yarlung Tsangpo. PRC have, therefore, addressed the UN in this matter to say that notwithstanding India and Bangladesh's objections, they are going ahead with the Project and have asked us to advise the two objecting countries to accept PRC's offer of compensation and PRC's decision to go ahead with the Project. Now, Gentlemen, what is your advice on the matter?" This was the President's Mr Robert Starr's opening address to the Security Council's members.

[The UNSC had been enlarged in 2025. Two new veto-wielding permanent members, Brazil and India had been added to the original five (China, France, Russia, the UK and the USA). The number of non-permanent members had also been increased from 10 to 14. The non-permanent members as on September 22 were Afghanistan, Albania, Algeria, Belgium, Canada, Ethiopia, Finland, Greece, Israel, Morocco, New Zealand, Oman, Peru and Thailand.—Author]

The President called upon the members from China, Russia, Thailand, the UK and the USA all of whom had signified their desire to speak, to do so in the order in which he named them.

All the speakers stated that the diversion of a major inter-national river against the original design of Nature was too serious a matter to be decided without very detailed examination by one or more expert committees. Though the 1997 Convention on Non-Navigational Uses of International Watercourses does give the Upper Riparian state right of ownership of the river that originates in that country, the right cannot be used to the total detriment of Lower Riparian states. They felt strongly that PRC's proposed water diversion project be examined by a Committee of legal experts and till then PRC should not take any unilateral action as it seems to be planning to.

The Thailand member made special reference to the case of the Salween river which flows from Tibet through Yunnan province of China to Myanmar and Thailand. If PRC plans to construct a dam across the Salween in Yunnan's earthquake prone region in order to divert the dammed water to the Chinese SNWD Project, the result will be disastrous for Thailand. He emphasized that waters or rivers should be treated as 'free' assets and not the sole property of the country where the rivers originate.

The USA member interjected that in his country, in a law suit (Wyoming vs. Colorado) the US Supreme Court had, under the 'doctrine of prior appropriation' ruled that an appropriator may remove water from its source and use it elsewhere for beneficial purposes. If this doctrine is applied, China may also divert its rivers for beneficial use to a 'reasonable' extent.

The discussion carried on in this manner without any consensus emerging. The President ruled that in view of the legal issues involved in what is actually interpretation of traditional practices, the Security Council could refer the matter to the International Court of Justice, The Hague, for proper interpretation of and codifying the Law of Riparian Rights expeditiously.

The Indian member proposed that till such time as the Court completes the codification of the Law on the subject, PRC be restricted by the Security Council from tampering with the direction of flow of Yarlung Tsangpo and other rivers flowing into South and South-East Asia from Tibet. The PRC member stated that no such restraint be placed on PRC in the matter of diversion of Yarlung Tsangpo waters on the grounds that it would constitute gross interference with the territorial sovereignty of PRC over every natural feature inside PRC's borders—and this includes the river. In any event, in this matter, which has been raised by the PRC to notify the UN that they are going ahead with the South to North Water diversion Project, for the Security Council to even consider a direction of restraint on PRC, would be entirely incorrect and should not be done. The President then ruled that the minutes should reflect that the matter has been discussed and will need to be referred to the International Court for interpreting and codifying the Law of Riparian Rights with no restrictions being placed on PRC. The meeting was then adjourned.

Chapter-13

Tibet Declares Independence

New Delhi

October 1, 2029

The Cabinet Committee on Political Affairs (CCPA) met at 7 RCR as scheduled on the 1st day of the month. In fact New Delhi had just now received news from The Hague that the International Court of Justice had found no reason to interfere with the 'Right ' of PRC to re-engineer the Yarlung Tsangpo to flow northwards instead of the present southward course at the Sino-Indian border. They averred that the 'Right' flowed automatically from the fact that Tibet was a part of PRC and this entitled her to enjoy all the rights inherent in this position of the Upper Riparian country under traditional law. They expressed the 'pious' hope that in exploiting their Right as the Upper Riparian, they should endeavour to minimize the effect on Lower Riparians who may be compensated for loss of large quantities of the waters of the river, in a suitable manner.

Though the Court's decision was a foregone conclusion, the Government of India, in consultation with its own legal luminaries examined the decision once again. Mr Justice Seshadri, Chief Justice of the Supreme Court of India stated, "The PRC derives the impugned 'Right' of being the 'Upper Riparian' through annexation of an independent country by military conquest in the 1950s. Unfortunately, India had acquiesced in the absorption of Tibet by PRC—reposing good faith in the benign character of the conqueror."

He continued, "Over a period of over 75 years, it has become transparent to all the world that the rule of PRC over Tibet was an 'enslavement ' of the people with a view to exploiting all their resources for the benefit of PRC and the detriment of Tibet." He said Tibetans are racially quite different from the Han people of China. PRC, being heavily populated, began to systematically settle its Han citizens on Tibetan land—so that Tibetans were increasingly crowded out of more productive lands. Where there was reluctance shown by Tibetans to vacate some tract of land for the Hans, fortuitous 'incidents' occurred, or were caused by PRC, to eliminate the reluctant Tibetan. This form of killing appears to have been systematized and may, quite properly, be termed 'state sponsored genocide'. This, coupled with the fact that pogroms have been launched periodically against the priestly class (lamas) and many places of worship (gompas) have been destroyed more than suggests that PRC wishes to wipe out Tibetan culture. An attempt has been made to hand pick the Panchen Lama and even then make him feeble and unable to look after the temporal aspects of the Tibetan's life. In time, perhaps, even worse may be attempted—i.e. to supplant the Dalai Lama—who is regarded as the spiritual Head of all Buddhists in Tibet and as God-incarnate."

"One other fact must be noted," Mr Justice Seshadri continued, "PRC is keen to keep Tibet under its rule for another, more materialistic reason—Minerals. Tibet is rich in copper, iron, chromites, Boron, Corundum, Crystal, Sulphur, Magnetite, Lithium and Mica. In addition, Tibetan plateau has significant deposits of Uranium, Gold, Zinc, Molybdenum, Lead, Silver and Caesium. PRC, therefore, has huge stakes to rule on in Tibet."

He concluded by saying, "Like the dread disease Cancer starts from a single cancerous cell and soon takes over and afflicts the whole body, the Chinese cancer has spread from being a border security activity to become the nemesis of Tibet. I fervently hope that our Government strikes the first blow against the Chinese cancer in Tibet by withdrawing its recognition of PRC as the 'master' of Tibet and restore to the Dalai Lama and his people what is rightfully theirs."

The CCPA was silent for a brief moment. Then, led by the Prime Minister, Mr Jagannath Das, the members broke into appreciative cheers with handclaps interspersed with calls of 'Bravo Sir' and 'down with China'. Some members actually left their seats to shake the learned Judge by the hand. The Prime Minister, as was his wont, raised his hands to bring the Committee to order again. There was much work to be done: garner support of the major powers, neighbours of China and as many other countries as possible within 96 hours of India making its declaration of 'Tibetan Freedom';

inform the Indian and Tibetan people of our decision to oust China from overlordship of Tibet; simultaneously inform the UN and the International Court of Justice at the Hague and other countries, not so far informed, of India's action; and last, but not the least, in a special audience with His Holiness, The Dalai Lama, a delegation led by the President of India and including the Prime Minister, External Affairs Minister, Home Minister and Defence Minister to ceremoniously call on to communicate India's correction of the blunder of the 1950s and seek his blessings for the Peace, Prosperity and Well-being of the People and Tibet.

New Delhi

October 2, Noon

In a televised address to the nation and carried live by television of almost every country except PRC, Indian Prime Minister Mr Jagannath Das delivered the following brief statement:

"Fellow Indians! Today is Gandhi Jayanthi, the birth anniversary of Mahatma Gandhi, the Father of the Nation. One hour ago, our country came to a standstill for one minute as a mark of respect to his memory."

Exactly one minute later, i.e. at 11.01 AM, the Speaker of the Tibetan Parliament in Exile made this proclamation on India TV:

> "With the blessings of His Holiness, The Dalai Lama, I declare Tibet to be a Sovereign, Democratic Republic free from the oppressive clutches of the People's Republic of China, which, for the last seven decades had our motherland groaning under their yoke. The Government of India has pledged to support us in every possible manner to make our Independence

meaningful and facilitate our moving back to our country. We are eternally grateful to India for helping us through our darkest days of exile to this glorious day of our Independence. On behalf of His Holiness, The Dalai Lama I convey His Blessings and Prayers to all fellow Tibetans and our steadfast friend India. May Tibet and India march together in eternal friendship to Peace and Prosperity."

Dacca, Bangladesh

October 2, 2029

The Bangladesh Cabinet met at the urgent summons of the Prime Minister in the Conference Room of the Bangla Parliament at noon. Addressing his colleagues the Prime Minister, Mr Shafiq ur Rehman said, "Tibet has declared its independence and India has accorded its formal recognition to the 'Sovereign, Democratic Republic of Tibet'. India has also informed the UNO and the International Court of Justice of this. Gentlemen, if Tibet is 'independent', there is no legal way open to the Chinese for diverting the waters of the Yarlung Tsangpo from South to North. We may be certain that the SNWD Project will be buried forever. Even in the July 31st Tripartite Meeting held at New Delhi, our Minister Mr Shahid ul Alam strongly supported India's refusal to countenance that Project. The Declaration of Independence by Tibet strengthens our stand against SNWD Project. It will be in the National interest if we too, without delay, recognise the Sovereign, Democratic Republic of Tibet and send cables to that effect to the Tibetan Government in Exile in India, India, the UN and China. Do you agree that I do so on behalf of our country immediately?"

There was a thunderous 'Aye' and the ministers expressed their joy by clapping in unison. Once the clapping was over, the Prime Minister said, "Thank you, Gentlemen. The cable to all concerned will be sent within half an hour."

The meeting was adjourned but not before everyone had a very hearty 'Tea' featuring the choicest Bangla sweets so famous the world over.

Chapter-14

China Reacts Angrily

Chengdu Military Area Command,

Operations Room

02 October, 1700 hrs

"The war alert orders were received just now," said the Chief Operations Officer. "I have ordered both 13 and 14 Corps to be prepared to occupy planned offensive operational positions all along the Sino-Indian border at 60 minutes notice. They will be ready to move by 1900 hrs."

General Chang, commanding Chengdu Military Area Command (MAC) nodded approvingly. He said, "Order the 14 Combined Corps to occupy their forward posture as required by Plan 'B' (attack on a wide front in Sikkim-Bhutan-South Tibet, i.e. Arunachal Pradesh as the Indians call it) by 0200 hrs tomorrow. Probing attacks may be carried out between 0200 hrs and 0430 hrs. If any of their selected objective areas are seen to be lightly held or unoccupied, they will forthwith attack and occupy them. All other troops to maintain aggressive forward posture and be prepared to attack their pre-designated objectives by 7 PM tomorrow. Are you clear so far?" The Chief Operations Officer said, "Yes, Sir. What about 13 Corps?"

General Chang nodded. "I am coming to that. 13 Corps is to position itself for attacks against Ladakh and the Central Sector. They should be at their battle locations by 0500 hrs tomorrow. They should be prepared for an all out attack in the Depsang Sector and Demchok-Chumar Sectors. They are to simultaneously carry out holding attacks in the Chushul Sector and Mana Sector in UP Area. All attacks/holding attacks are to start tomorrow night with the holding attacks going in first and the main attack later. Operations to be completed within 72 hours thereafter, i.e. by 6 October first light."

"The two combined Corps have adequate organic reserves. Overall theatre reserves will be provided by 21 Corps ex Lanzhou Military Area, with the task of reinforcing either 13 or 14 Combined Corps with up to two divisions each. The balance of 27 and 47 Corps will be held under arrangements of PLAA HQ."

General Chang was an experienced commander. His plans were generally simple and uncomplicated. His technique was to attack with overwhelming force and use reserves to maintain momentum. Balance in operations was usually sought to be attained by using the theatre reserves.

The plans against India were simple and adequate troops were earmarked for each. However, what he saw of the Indian Artillery in Nathula-Jelepla earlier on made him use more troops than he would have normally done. He also toyed with the idea of asking the PLA GHQ to allot some short range (up to 200kms) weapons from PLA Second Artillery—the nuclear artillery. With these at his back he was confident that Chengdu MAC will be successful in all its missions. Ruminating on these lines, General Chang walked through the Military Area of Chengdu to his three roomed house on Jasmine Avenue.

Arunachal Pradesh, Bhutan, Sikkim Sector

Operations of 14 Combined Corps

October 03-04 (First Light)

14 Combined Corps arrived in the intended battle zone between 1900 hrs and 2300 hrs on 02 October. A division each deployed itself in forward assembly areas, their assigned objectives being Bomdila and Walong. Both sectors were found to be heavily defended. Attempts to probe the flanks for gaps or weaknesses indicated that the Indians had taken adequate care to see that their flanks are not turned. The Divisional Commander therefore decided to attack in overwhelming strength on night October 3/4 with very heavy artillery preparation. In the event, as soon as the Chinese artillery opened fire, an Indian riposte in the form of concentrated heavy calibre gun and rocket fire ensued. Here again, the extensive use of thermo-baric ammunition broke the morale of the soldiers who dreaded the combination of intense heat, blast and suction of air that this type of ammunition produces. The attacks in both objective areas were called off after very heavy casualties were sustained by the Chinese.

The Divisional Commander asked for close air support from early morning of October 4 to soften up the defences and enable the attacker to 'punch a hole' through them. Air to air combat ensued with the Chinese aircraft, due to their airfields being at altitudes of 14,000 feet or so, carrying only a fraction of their normal ammunition load at take off. The IAF had no such difficulty and was able to completely blunt PLAAF's considerable air power. To sum up the battle so far, The PLA supported by PLAAF failed to achieve even a foothold in the assigned objective areas. Their casualty figures were enormous for such a brief period of fighting—PLA had 460 including 140 soldiers killed and PLAAF lost six fighter aircraft and had two airfields put out of action for an estimated 48 hours.

A very similar story was being played out in the Ladakh and Central Sectors where 13 Combined Corps, despite some initial success in the Depsang Plateau area were pushed back across the border by multi-barrelled rocket fire. They also had the mortification of having their rear echelon attacked by what seemed to be excellently trained and equipped Tibetan Ski troops. In fact the Tibetan Commando group, in its maiden battle, set a major supply dump on fire besides destroying over 30 load carrying vehicles. It was, indeed, a very bad day for PLA and PLAAF and an excellent one for Tibetan Commandos and Indian formations.

Concurrent with the fighting by regulars, not to be left behind and contribute their mite to the common cause, armed Uyghurs and Nei Monggol guerrillas sniped at Chinese foot and vehicular movement and blew up one culvert on the Xinjiang Highway. The Nei Monggols carried out a petrol bomb attack on the Police Station manned by the Chinese and destroyed one fire tender which had come to put out the blaze.

The cumulative result of all these initial reverses on the Chinese Government was to take the matter to the UN

Security Council. After three hours of debate, the UNSC called for both sides to cease by 1700 hrs, 04 October all forms of provocative military and covert actions as well as pull back their respective troops to a distance of 100 kilometres on their own side of the border. Russia and India 'vetoed' the UNSC Resolution Number 3979 calling for ceasefire and withdrawal of both belligerents. India, however, stated that it may agree to comply with the UNSC resolution provided (a) China quits Tibet by October 15 and (b) China stops all work on the SNWD Project forthwith—this to be verified on ground by a UN appointed neutral observer. The session ended with the Chinese representative staging a walkout with the members of his delegation.

At this time—October 4, 1400 hrs New York time, an Indian surveillance satellite picked up the movement of short range elements of China's Second Artillery. This sighting was confirmed by Russia, Japan and Taiwan. The UN, addressing the Chinese Government directly, demanded an immediate end to this 'sabre rattling'. USA, Russia, UK and France also made a similar demand. At this time, Tibetan commando troops made a number of bold attacks on Chinese vehicular movements. Their crowning achievement was the taking over of a Chinese load carrying lorry, loading it up with high explosives from a secret hoard, boldly driving up to the entrance of 3,000 metre long Galongla tunnel on the Metok Road and blowing it up causing closure of the tunnel for over 12 hours. Three Tibetan commandos lost their lives in this daring exploit. Elsewhere too, Tibetan commando activity was in evidence. The Gormo-Lhasa Railway line was temporarily closed when during the night of October 4/5, explosives were used to blow up a two metre section of the railway. All this caused considerable alarm to the Chinese population settled in Tibet, some of whom managed to leave Tibet in a returning military convoy to safer areas in China.

Renewing their attacks, the Chinese launched daring daylight regimental attacks at the airfield at Daulat Beg Oldi and on a feature called Trig Height both in the Depsang Plateau. It was touch and go at the DBO Airfield as the Chinese used tanks and armoured personnel carriers and were at the fencing of the Airfield when IAF Sukhoi appeared on the scene and wreaked havoc with the intruding tanks and the APCs. The battlefield was cleared of any live enemy within 15 minutes of the arrival of IAF aircraft on the scene.

At the Trig Height, however, the Chinese had moved very carefully through folds in the ground on foot and approached to within 1000metres of the Indian defences. The Artillery observer on Trig Height thereafter took over the battle—literally—as he ordered two multi barrel Rocket batteries to fire two salvoes each in less than eight minutes, mowing down the brave attackers. Perhaps, the Chinese had forgotten that daylight attack by Infantry across open country is not to be attempted unless the attacker is suicidal-minded. In the event, between DBO and Trig Heights, the Chinese lost over 180 soldiers killed or wounded and 250 soldiers captured with weapons and ammunition. They also lost six artillery guns—destroyed by our air attacks.

The UNSC again met in an emergency session to bring to an end the fighting which seemed to be getting more intense. Their resolution No 3980 was passed calling for a ceasefire by all combatants and for India and China to enter into direct negotiations facilitated by the UN Secretary General. Both India and China agreed to the ceasefire and to send their Foreign Ministers to UN HQ at New York for one-to-one talks with the Secretary General helping them to get over bottlenecks. Matters appeared to be going well by all accounts till a coded message was brought in by our Ambassador in USA to our Foreign Minister. The gist of the message was that a Joint Indo-Tibetan Long range Patrol had found positive evidence of intended use of nuclear explosives by the Chinese to blast a channel through a major hill which lay on their selected alignment of the diverted Yarlung Tsangpo. The Chinese had almost completed the boring of the tunnel which was being dug to serve as the site for placement of the nuclear explosive device. The message stated that the nuclear explosives themselves were stored in a cave some 500 metres away. The message went on to say that the mechanical drilling of the nuclear site was going on and had penetrated some 100 metres into the mountain at a depth of 30 metres. The LRP asked for guidance from the Defence Minister and had been told to use conventional explosives carried for the purpose to close the entry to the tunnel while the men and their machines are trapped inside the partly dug tunnel. The patrol had done as directed and had moved away from the area to safety. The tunnellers, sadly, must be presumed to have died of asphyxiation 100 metres in and 30 metres from the top of the mountain they were tunnelling.

The talks between the Indian and Chinese Foreign Ministers were continuing in fits and starts—each side requesting instructions from their principals in New Delhi and Beijing. There was no perceptible progress as the talks meandered here and there and returned to what the first question to be decided was—who was to disengage first, what distances should the two sides fall back to, what measures of surveillances are required to ensure neither side violates the ceasefire and so on.

Meanwhile, in Chinese controlled Nei Monggol (Inner Mongolia), a freedom movement had sprung up. Inspired by activists of Southern Mongolian Human Rights Information Centre (SMHRIC), the movement embarked on organised violence against Han Chinese settled in Nei Monggol. Small groups of two or three men armed with modern weapons such as automatic rifles, machine pistols, rocket launchers and even ground-to-air missiles became so active that Chinese Hans had been ordered by Beijing to stay in groups of four or five and not venture out after dark. Yet, despite these orders, the Nei Monggols who were formerly peaceful herders tending their cattle, now sought out and killed Hans. Alarmed at the high rate of attrition of Hans in Nei Monggol, a Chinese Army Division was dispatched to restore law and order. Unfortunately for this Division, their route was interrupted by numerous blasted bridges, ambushes in strength and taking of prisoners by the Mongols. Airborne troops were then ordered to land in Nei Monggol. They were greeted by excellent ack-ack weapons—shoulder fired missiles—clearly made in Russia. The Chinese protested to Russia but were given an evasive reply. However, they made it clear that their sympathies and support are for the Nei Monggols.

We have already seen what the Uyghurs did to the Chinese in Urumqi and have had a sampling of the non-herder kind of activity of the Nei Monggols. We now turn to Tibet, or rather the Sovereign Democratic Republic of Tibet. So far only India and Bangladesh had recognised their independence. The Tibetan Parliament in Exile interacted with the Government of India and sought help for raising an 'Independent Tibetan Army'. This help and much more than what they asked for was given by India. A place to raise the 'Army', funds, weapons and equipment, ammunition and explosives, all-terrain vehicles and specialised training—all these were given by India for raising the 'Independent Tibetan Army'.

We need not go further into the 'birth pangs' and 'building blocks' of the Independent Tibetan Army (ITA). Suffice it to say that ITA was a mission driven force. That mission was the re-capture of the Tibetan capital Lhasa—ITA as raised by mid-2029 consisted of HQ ITA and four 'Battle Groups', each consisting of four battalions of hand-picked, robust and courageous Himalayan troops. One battalion in each Battle Group was also trained in air-borne operations. They were equipped with the latest weaponry and were capable of day/night and all weather operations including on skis. They trained, day in and day out, for over one year for carrying out one single operation—recapture of Lhasa. With this kind of training and their patriotic fervour, they were bound to be successful in their Mission.

One point needs to be clarified: How well did the ITA troops know the layout and topography of Lhasa? Quite simply answered? As well as a person who has lived all his life in that city. With the help of the IAF reconnaissance flights, very high resolution satellite imagery (accurate to the nearest yard!) and by 3-D imagery of key buildings like the Potala Palace, everyone in the Battle Groups knew Lhasa even better than one born and brought up there. It is considered important to mention all this as the recapture of Lhasa is vital for making sure that China's dastardly SNWD Project does not take place. Lhasa must become the Capital of Free Tibet.

The raising of the ITA was kept a closely guarded secret. However, during the course of the fighting in October, the Chinese appeared to have learnt of this Tibetan Army. However, they did not have any idea of what it was capable of achieving. The moment of Truth will soon come and they will know all!

Chapter-15

Teetering on the Edge

Beijing October 12

President's Residence, Noon

President Hong was very unhappy. He had staked the future of the country on one project—SNWD Project. Now it seems a non-starter. The Bayankala Mountains acted as an insuperable barrier to the Northward diversion of Yarlung Tsangpo. Despite their best efforts the Seismologists, Hydro-Engineers, and Scientists had failed to find even one alignment in the Bayankala earthquake region for the Yarlung Tsangpo to flow north. Even before the Bayankala barrier was reached, there was a major setback; a tunnel was required to be bored at a depth of 30 metres through another mountain straddling the chosen alignment of the Yarlung Tsangpo. The work was well under control and the place for detonating the nuclear explosive had been reached about 100 metres into the mountain. And a party of saboteurs closed the entrance to the tunnel using explosives with the tunnel diggers and their machines trapped in the bosom of the mountain forever. First the earthquake zone and now this—President Hong shook his head—no, he was very unhappy.

Other events too must be added to his tally of woes. The Uyghur blackmail, the Tibetan sabotage of the new Road linking Bomi and Metok Counties by Tibetan Special Forces personnel, the attacks on Han Chinese in Nei Monggol, the difficulties experienced by first the Infantry division and later the Airborne formation (sent to control the situation) at the hands of Nei Monggols, the Declaration of Independence by Tibet, our unhappy experience in the early October war and so on..."My cup of misery overflows" said the President waving his hand in a dramatic gesture and knocking down his pot of green tea..."How cruel life can be?" he asked.

Just then his Aide came in to announce the arrival of key members of the Government and some senior party leaders as desired by him.

The group he had called today were the most powerful persons in all China. Mr Hong wished to share his miseries and consequent plans with them. Perhaps someone among them might even throw up a good idea, though in his present mood President Hong did not believe anything good will come out of this meeting.

He set the ball rolling by recounting all the recent events that had given him great unhappiness. He then proceeded to give out his determination to overcome all these problems in his own way. His short speech was pithy, rhetorical, boastful and somewhat malevolent. He said:

- We shall fight it out with all our strength and weapons including nuclear weapons.
- We shall enforce such a peace in Xinjiang, Tibet and Nei Monggol that the World will tremble at the very thought of fighting China.
- The Indians, who initiated, inspired, armed and directed all this Anti-China activity will be punished with no mercy shown to them.
- The other world powers, i.e. USA and Russia, Japan and Taiwan must withdraw their support for the India-inspired rebellions and use their economic power to bring India to its knees.

Then, as though overcome by his own emotions, he waved the assembled notables away. They were all puzzled and disturbed. One among them, Fang Yamen, Minister for Railways was so stunned that he wanted to share it with someone or other or his head would burst. The first person he met was the USA qualified physical culture expert, Ho Liangku. He gushed out what had transpired at the meeting. Ho told him to try and forget what he had heard, for the President was probably having a bad day. Fang, somewhat relieved at having unburdened himself, went to his bachelor's quarters. Unfortunately, at that very instant, Ho Liangku, who was A CIA agent, was briefing his boss at Langley, USA about what President Hong had said barely half an hour ago. He spoke in Yiddish interspersing his sentences with words from a physical culturist's repertoire so that a chance eavesdropper may not get suspicious of the call to the USA. His boss immediately had the entire speech of President Hong passed on to the President of the United States (POTUS).

At about 6 PM, a strongly worded message from POTUS was received by President Hong. What he heard convinced him that someone who had attended the meeting had leaked the entire contents to somehow reach the ears of POTUS within six hours. A 'witch hunt' was immediately started to trace the culprit. And it did not require much of a 'witch hunt' either for Fang, who was the third person to be questioned, broke down and confessed immediately. He was shot by a firing squad at dawn on October 13—the very next day. Ho Liangku managed to escape to Taiwan the next day.

POTUS took a very serious view of the PRC President's decision and warned him of grave consequences. He also consulted the Russian President, the Prime Minister of UK and the UN Secretary General before he spoke to Mr Hong. Others whom the POTUS had consulted also sent a similar message to PRC: the British—politely but firmly, the Russian—roughly and the Secretary General—conveying in a diplomatic way that as a Permanent Member of the Security Council, he trusted that PRC will do nothing to lower the dignity of the UNO.

At 8 PM, President Hong and Premier Lung in a joint television appearance said, "We have no quarrel with the USA or Britain, as yet. We are aware of our rights and duties as a Permanent Member of the UN. We need no advice on this issue. A country that does need this advice is also a Permanent Member—India. They are shamelessly trampling on everything the UN stands for and, to make matters worse, they are inciting our provinces in China to rebel. We shall not countenance this. Our warning to them is final and clear: STOP your aggression against PRC; STOP interfering in our internal affairs; or, face the wrath of Mighty China who will crush you with conventional as well as with nuclear weapons."

Clearly China is teetering 'on the edge of the Rubicon'.

A major war against India is inevitable and probably imminent.

New Delhi,

Prime Minister's Residence, 2100 hrs, October 12

The Cabinet Committee on Security assembled in an 'emergency' meeting at 7 RCR. The Prime Minister, looking relaxed and, surprisingly, happy, said to the members of the Committee, " Just as we had foreseen! Hong has been 'stung' and seems to be in a foul mood. We now need to get our people organised for the nuclear war Hong has threatened to unleash on us. Does anyone amongst you have any questions to ask about our getting ready for N-war?"

No one had any question as the country had done nearly three dozen 'Nuclear War Imminent' (NWI) Drills since we went nuclear at the turn of the century. Initially, one Drill was carried out every alternate year but since the year 22, NWI Drills had been conducted twice a year—the last one having concluded in June 2029. So, there was no confusion in India. NWI Drills had been designed to enable every section of the People and Government to function with no loss of efficiency under conditions of nuclear war. Since no one had any doubt, the PM asked the Cabinet Secretary to issue codeword 'Bajrang' with effect from 6 AM, October 14. The Cabinet Secretary repeated back "Bajrang with effect from 6 AM October 14." He then went off to the Cypher Room to issue the NWI Codeword.

A word about Bajrang. This codeword is issued when nuclear war is imminent to all echelons of Central and State Governments, the Armed Forces, Civil Defence Organisations, National Disaster Relief Organisation, Atomic Energy Commission and every hospital and medical facility in the country. Deep underground shelters had already been constructed a kilometer or so away from likely nuclear targets. These robust concrete and steel structures were kept stocked with food, water, medical supplies and sufficient wherewithal to enable the occupants to function for a full year. Artificial illumination, own air, water and recycling plants for these, class rooms and sports facilities for younger people had been arranged. A close circuit television for news and entertainment programmes was also installed and could be accessed by everyone living underground. An excellent Library too had been catered for as well as a small online newspaper called 'Bajrang' giving the latest news, sports scores, important happenings and so on, on the underground computer network. All in all, the underground shelters replicated over-ground life to a considerable extent.

India's strategic forces also had made full preparations for a major war against China. Road and rail mobile nuclear armed missiles deployed in pre-designated hides; our submarines with their ICBMs would already have put to sea some time before the storm broke. Further, all major cities, population centres, production centres and other vulnerable areas were brought within the protective umbrella of the National Anti-Missile Shield.

All key Government, command and communications centres had already been moved to alternative war time locations. As far as the Armed Forces were concerned, it was 'battle stations' with full nuclear protection methods being fully employed. There was no panic in the country. India was fully prepared to take on the Chinese and defeat them.

The Chinese threat over television evoked great excitement throughout the world. There was a great deal of support for India. Apart from political pronouncements by leaders of various countries, the USA, Russia, the UK, Japan, France, Germany, Brazil, Republic of Korea, Vietnam and many others went on full scale battle alert. The fleets of the Great Powers put out to sea with their nuclear weaponry. All Satellite Surveillance stations were focused on China and her sole ally North Korea. India was kept informed of every single move of the Chinese by these countries. All this was highly appreciated by India.

New Delhi, October 14, Noon

Doordarshan Studios

Since 6 AM the 'flier' "Prime Minister will address the Nation at 12 hrs" was carried with every DD programme, at the stroke of mid day, everyone in India and perhaps in many other parts of the world people's attentions was riveted to the TV screen. "'The Prime Minister Mr Jagannath Das will now address the Nation," the Announcer said. When he started speaking almost everyone remarked on how different his speech was, when compared with the rather bellicose speech of his Chinese counterpart. Mr Das spoke in a calm, measured tone. There was no pugnacity or bravado in his words—maybe there was a hint of sadness at the turn of events. He said:

"Fellow Indians! The President of the Peoples Republic of China has thrown us the gauntlet and threatened us with nuclear war if we continued our 'aggression' as he put it, against his country. India has taken note of his threat. All I wish to tell China is that this is not 1962 but 2029. They forget that today, India is the world's largest economy and has equipped and trained her Armed forces to be second to none in the world. Our Science and technology are keeping pace—in fact, are even surging ahead of some of the best in the field. Our people are young—more than half of us Indians are below 30 years of age. These are some facts which the Chinese will do well to remember. If they are reckless enough to make war on us, it will be a most regrettable decision on their part. I wish to say no more except that we are ready. And to you, fellow Indians, I ask you to be stout of heart, resolute in every contingency and with the Grace of the Almighty, be confident that we shall prevail. Jai Hind!"

Chapter-16

UN Emergency Session

UN Headquarters, New York, October 14, 1300 hrs

Emergency Session of UNSC

Alarmed at the grave situation that had arisen between the two most populous and powerful nations on earth, the Secretary General convened an emergency meeting of the Security Council to start at 0900 hrs on October 15. He also warned the President of the UN General Assembly that it may become necessary to convene a 'Uniting for Peace' General Assembly session if the UNSC meeting results in no action due to exercise of 'veto' power by one or more of the members attending. There was a general air of pessimism the world over and all the nations of the world braced themselves for facing a Nuclear Armageddon.

Opening Shots, Naval Clash in South China Sea

30 NM South of Hainan, 1700 hrs, October 14

INS Brahmaputra sailing due east to rendezvous with a flotilla of Indian Navy ships some 100 Nm to eastwards, picked up on radar the approach at high speed of an aircraft towards her. The unknown aircraft, which was at almost 10,000 feet altitude suddenly went into a dive and rapidly approached the position of *INS Brahmaputra.* At about 2 kilometres from the Indian ship, the unknown aircraft arrested its dive and pulled up at a steep angle. INS *Brahmaputra,* already in evasive action, detected a large bomb or missile heading for the ship. One Barak missile was ordered to be fired. It was successful in hitting the hostile weapon which exploded with thunderous noise. The debris from the exploded weapon were collected and examined. It was unmistakably a Chinese weapon and designed to destroy the Indian ship. The hostile aircraft disappeared even from radar after delivering its attack at very high speed.

The flotilla of IN ships which *INS Brahmaputra* was supposed to join had followed the brief action which involved our ship and its excellent response. The attacker had gone on without landing at Hainan probably to Kunming airbase. *INS Brahmaputra* was ordered to join the flotilla as planned and not initiate a counter-attack against Hainan or any other target as officially the war had not yet started despite the rather inept and infructuous Chinese attack. Coming as the instruction did from the Captain of *INS Vikramadithya* where the fleet commander Vice Admiral Rajan was aboard, *INS Brahmaputra* did as directed.

Line of Actual Control Violated, Ladakh

Area Chumar, Eastern Ladakh, 1900 hrs, October 14

1 Jat, responsible for the defence of the Chumar-Tible-Monkhar Sector was fully aware of the Chinese interest in the Chumar area. Clearly, if they captured the 1 Jat positions, they could link up with a thrust from Fukche and capture Demchok from the rear. CO 1 Jat, had told his battalion, "This is a task for an ace battalion and that is why Jat Balwan has been tasked to do it." The Battalion's morale could not be higher.

At about 1900 hrs, battlefield surveillance radars at Monkhar forward and Tible picked up two Company sized columns of Chinese moving tactically towards Chumar. Even at a distance of 500 metres from the border the CO did not order the troops to fire. After the war, when he was asked why he held back from firing even though the enemy was clearly coming for his positions, he said with a grin, "If I had done that, you will blame me for starting the War! In any case when the first assault wave of the Chinese crossed the LAC, we opened fire rather effectively. 6 Chinese soldiers were killed by the combined fire of our soldiers and Artillery. The Chinese were allowed to pick up their wounded lying on their side of the LAC while those who were wounded on our side of the LAC, 24 of them, were tended to by 1 Jat at their Regimental Aid Post.

Lhasa, Tibet

Power Station, 2100 hrs, October 14

The engineer in charge of the Power Station for the night, Ho Yilin, was very uneasy. The men on duty too were strangely restive. It was as if something unexpected was about to happen. At 9 PM precisely, there was an explosion which seemed to have come from the interior of the huge transformer which stepped down the received power from 1000 Kilovolts to a manageable 220 volts. The Power Station and all of Lhasa were plunged into darkness. And then, the shooting started—clearly the stuttering of Kalashnikovs - at least 20-30 of them - in the city bus station. There was a lot of shouting in Tibetan vernacular asking people not to be afraid but get down from two buses which were ready to move. The passengers got down—among them two PLA soldiers in uniform. The soldiers were shot and killed immediately. The buses were emptied in less than a minute. Suddenly, a group of Tibetans who were in the dark area near the buses, their faces blackened in camouflage, carrying their Kalashnikovs and between every two men, a large sack, broke cover. "There were 48 men" said the hapless Tibetan policeman.

The 48 men with 24 sacks boarded the two buses and whispered some 'magic words' in Tibetan to the two florid faced drivers. The drivers grinned hugely, threw a mock salute and drove on to the Norbulinka Road, past the Exhibition Hall to Potala Palace. Lhasa was still in total darkness.

There was a flurry of activity from the men who had commandeered the two buses when the vehicles stopped having driven up the narrow path to the ticketing office. They sprinted up the steps to the Red Palace and thence to the White Palace. Eight men were

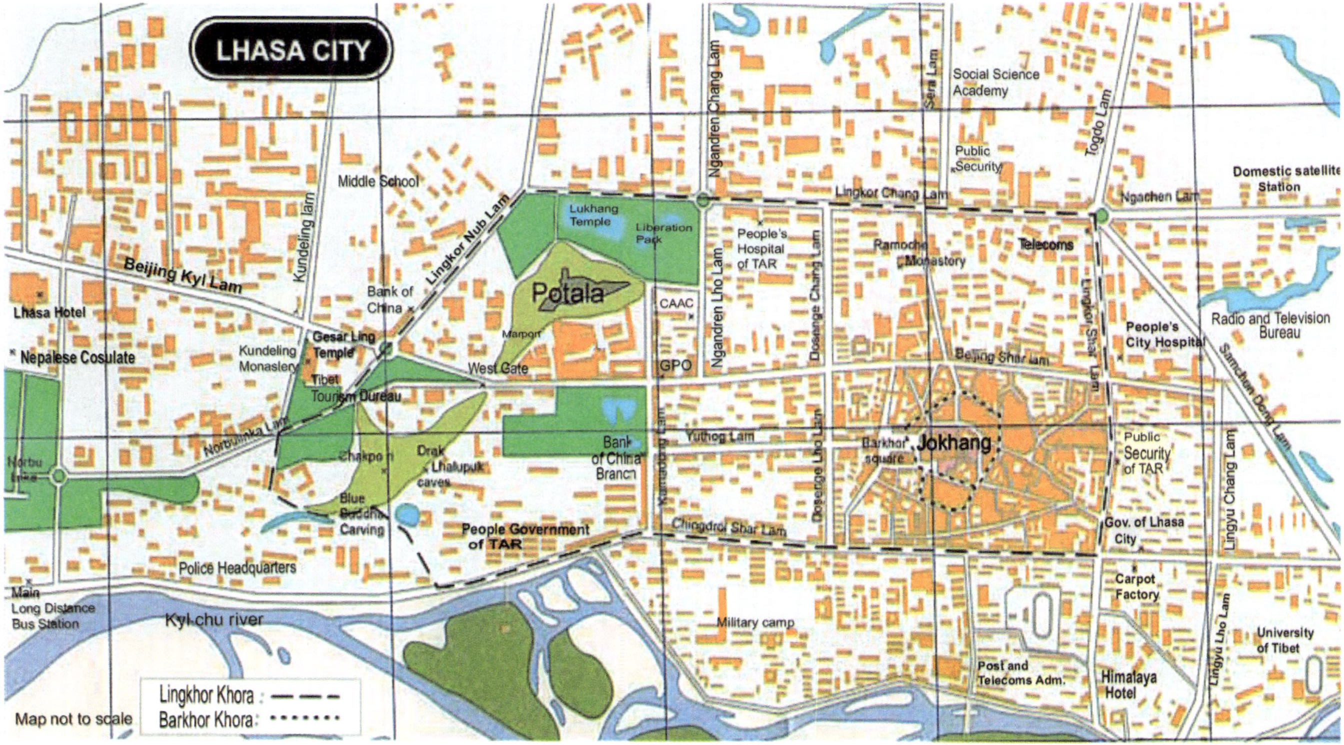
LHASA CITY
Social Science Academy
Public Security
Domestic satellite Station
Middle School
Sera Lam
Togdo Lam
Ngandren Chang Lam
Lingkor Chang Lam
Ngachen Lam
Lukhang Temple
Liberation Park
People's Hospital of TAR
Ramoche Monastery
Telecoms
Kundeling lam
Lingkor Nub Lam
Beijing Kyi Lam
Bank of China
Potala
CAAC
Ngandren Lho Lam
Dosenge Chang Lam
Lingkor Shar Lam
People's City Hospital
Radio and Television Bureau
Lhasa Hotel
Nepalese Cosulate
Gesar Ling Temple
Kundeling Monastery
Marpori
West Gate
GPO
Beijing Shar lam
Samchen Dong Lam
Tibet Tourism Bureau
Norbulinka Lam
Norbu linka
Chakpori
Drak Lhalupuk caves
Bank of China Branch
Yuthog Lam
Dosenge Lho Lam
Barkhor square
Jokhang
Public Security of TAR
Lingyu Chang Lam
Blue Buddha Carving
People Government of TAR
Chingdrol Shar Lam
Gov. of Lhasa City
Police Headquarters
Main Long Distance Bus Station
Kyi-chu river
Military camp
Carpet Factory
Lingyu Lho Lam
University of Tibet
Post and Telecoms Adm.
Himalaya Hotel
Lingkhor Khora :
Barkhor Khora :
Map not to scale

A View of Potala Palace, Lhasa

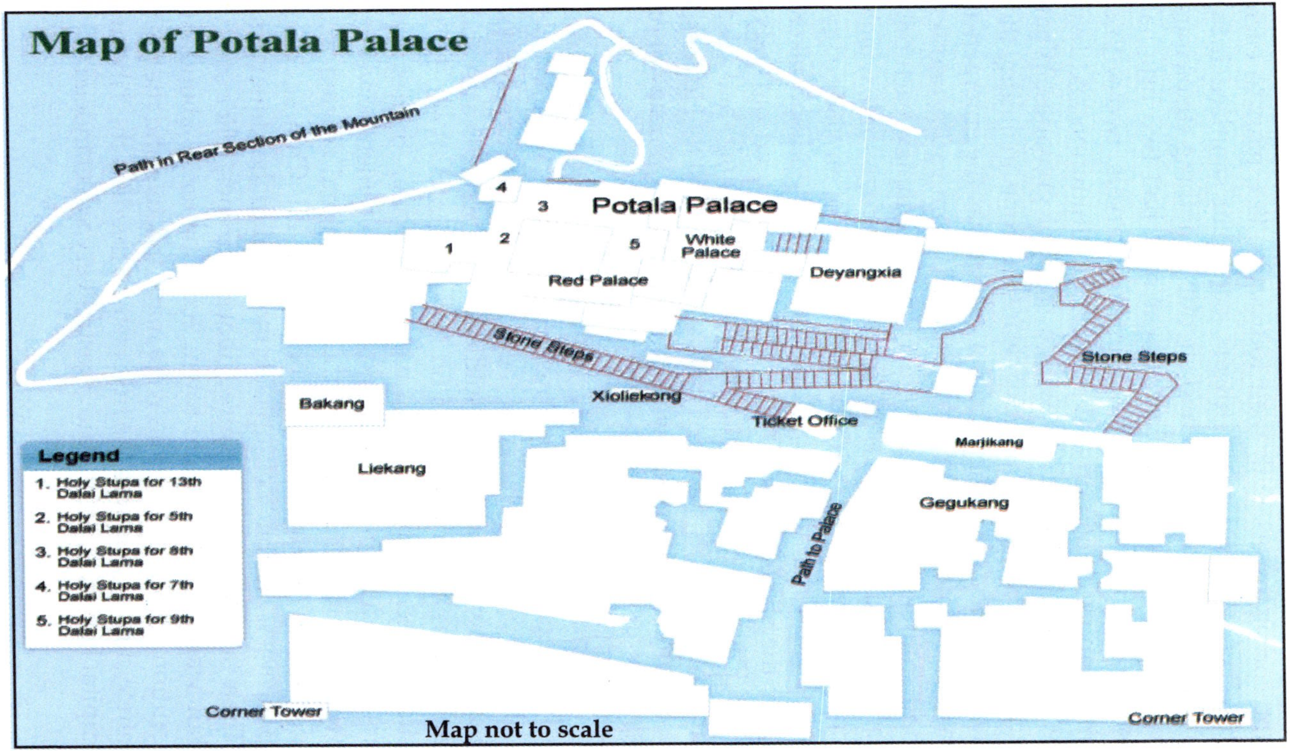
Map of Potala Palace
Path in Rear Section of the Mountain
Potala Palace
1
2
3
4
5
White Palace
Red Palace
Deyangxia
Stone Steps
Stone Steps
Xioliekong
Ticket Office
Bakang
Liekang
Marjikang
Gegukang
Path to Palace
Legend
1. Holy Stupa for 13th Dalai Lama
2. Holy Stupa for 5th Dalai Lama
3. Holy Stupa for 8th Dalai Lama
4. Holy Stupa for 7th Dalai Lama
5. Holy Stupa for 9th Dalai Lama
Corner Tower
Corner Tower
Map not to scale

the corner towers with their four sacks, two pairs to each tower. On arrival at the towers, each pair sanitised it by making a cautious climb and shooting anything suspicious with a silenced pistol. Each tower now had two original occupants (now dead) and four new arrivals, two with a medium machine gun and 8 belts of ammunition and two with grenade firing rifles with a stock of grenades. What they expected to fight was not clear to anyone, including the new arrivals. What they did not expect was the emergence of Tibetan men, women, boys and girls from various nooks and crannies of the huge Potala Palace Complex, each one greeting the new arrivals in Tibetan and a huge smile which conveyed what they felt, without the help of any language. They knew that their own kind had arrived and had taken over the sacred Potala Palace. One of them, an old lady, asked whether His Holiness, the Dalai Lama had also arrived. She was told in Tibetan, " Mother! His Holiness will come to Lhasa once we have chased the Chinese out of Tibet."

By midnight, electricity had been restored in Lhasa. Chinese personnel in the Power Station were arrested and Tibetans placed in charge of the station. There was at least a battalion worth of Chinese soldiers in the Stadium area and another in a set of barracks on Jingzhoi Road, West. They did not seem to be aware of the momentous activities that took place a couple of hours ago. Lhasa policemen, however, were very quick in reading the situation and reacted like patriotic Tibetans should—locked up all Chinese Han policemen in the lock-ups of their police headquarters. Their families were reassured about their men folk's safety but warned not to leave town. As a matter of abundant caution, all telephone lines were made inactive and the post office closed. This was the first taste of freedom the Tibetan capital had since 1959. And it tasted very sweet indeed.

United Nations Headquarters, 15 October, 0900 hrs

Emergency Meeting of the UN Security Council

Mr Robert Starr, the Secretary General ushered Mr Dmitri Pavlov to the Presidential Chair and whispered to him as he assumed the role of President 'Good Luck, Dmitri, you will have to play your best Chess at this meeting to keep China and India from plunging the World into a nuclear war.' Dmitri, probably the only diplomat who became a Grandmaster and for three years held the World Title for Chess, shook hands with Starr and signalled the start of the Emergency Meeting with these words:

"We meet today to prevent a cataclysmic war from breaking out between PRC and India, two of our permanent members, over a river water sharing dispute which got complicated by the involvement of countries neighbouring these two countries, fighting for their own felt needs and rights. PRC and India have adopted diametrically opposite positions on both the main issue, i.e. water sharing and subsidiary issues of other nations' aspirations. The experience, wisdom and goodwill of all of us will be tested in this session. If, as I hope, we succeed, a golden era of mutual compromise and consideration for the rights and aspirations of all countries, great or small, will be ushered in. Should, God forbid, we prove ourself to be incapable of doing so, the World may be plunged into a calamitous war, one that may spell the end of Civilisation. I pray that all of us will find the wisdom, courage and humanity to arrive at a positive result at the end of our deliberations here."

He then called upon the representatives of the two major contending parties to espouse their respective complaints and counter-complaints/replies. He called upon the PRC to state their case.

Mr Chai Zemin, the PRC representative rose and briefly bowed to the other delegates. He looked pugnacious, self assured and somewhat overconfident of the merits of his country's case. The gist of his address is given below:

- PRC's population in 2030 is expected to be 1.5 billion people, i.e. 22 per cent of the world's population.
- PRC has only 8 per cent of the world's fresh water to meet the requirements of 22 per cent of the world's population.
- Even this 8 per cent is unevenly distributed keeping in mind the distribution of population. Southern China with 85 million population has 8 per cent of China's water, whereas Northern China with 55 million population has 2 per cent only.
- In order to correct this lopsided distribution of fresh water, it was proposed to divert some waters from South flowing rivers towards the North.
- The river Yarlung Tsangpo has the maximum flow out of the South flowing rivers and its diversion along with that of the Salween and Mekong rivers was conceived to meet the requirements of North China.
- This, in essence is the South to North Water Diversion project (SNWD Project).
- India, into which the Yarlung Tsangpo flows first after its 2057 km flow through the Chinese province of Tibet, has objected to this SNWD Project on the grounds that they will be hard hit by this diversion as India's major river in the affected area, i.e. Ganges will lose 30 per cent of its water which it gets when the Yarlung Tsangpo (called Brahmaputra in India) joins the Ganges as its major tributary. Bangladesh further downstream will also be affected to some

extent.

- We discussed this SNWD Project with India and Bangladesh ministers at a conference convened at our request at New Delhi on July 31, this year. We accepted that there would be some reduction of water flow in India's Ganges and Bangladesh which calls the same Ganges by other names. We offered to consider a compensation package to make up for the notional crop loss, ecological damage and so on.
- Unfortunately, having heard our case and offer of compensation, India, very summarily rejected our offer and abruptly concluded the meeting. Bangladesh sided with India in this action.

Mr Chai Zemin said that this is the first of their complaints and may be dealt with before the Council hears the remaining complaints against India—these being inciting Chinese provinces to revolt and large scale sabotage and anti-Chinese activities in their territory.

After some discussion with his staff and advisors in the privacy of a separate chamber, the President Dmitri Pavlov agreed to the Chinese request and asked India, the country most affected by the complaint to reply to the issues agitated by the Chinese.

The Indian representative, Mr Surya Prakash, then took the floor. He said he had no problem in accepting the fact that China is a water stressed country and the quantum availability of fresh water for North China is less than that for South China, per capita. However, the data cited by the Chinese representative are selectively incomplete and grossly misleading. "This", he said, "is the problem with people and countries who believe that they live alone on planet Earth and there are no other countries or people sharing the living space, natural resources, air and water with them."

Mr Chai Zemin jumped to his feet to interrupt but the President Dmitri Pavlov glared at him so intensely that Mr Chai quickly resumed his seat. [Incidentally, Dmitri Pavlov's glare used to have this effect on his Chess opponents some commentators calling it 'mesmeric', others 'compelling' and yet others 'like a *karate* chop to the head].

Mr Surya Prakash continued, "Statistics are a lying jade as the saying goes. Let us see what the comparison is in terms of water availability for India which has 18 per cent of the World's population and only 4.5 per cent of its water supply. As it stands today, India is much worse off than China in terms of water availability—even after making allowance for 40 per cent of China's water supply being 'unsuitable for drinking, industry and agriculture'. So why should China seek to benefit at India's expense? Unless China is the only country on Earth, such a flawed logic must be regarded as only self serving and deserves to be rejected by all who believe that 22 per cent population does not entitle one to misappropriate the water of the neighbouring 18 per cent or any other human being whatsoever. May I share a small interchange between a school boy and his class teacher who told him that China's name in Chinese is 'Chung Guo' meaning the Central Kingdom. The school boy was surprised. He said, "China is a part of Asia, which is a large continent and China is in the eastern part of it. Then there are other continents, Europe, the Americas, Africa, Australia and so on. So, is China in the middle of it all?" the teacher mollified the schoolboy and said "do not take the name seriously—it was meant to be a joke." Mr Chai Zemin sprang up to his feet and spluttered—at a loss for words. Mr Dmitri Pavlov looked at Mr Surya Prakash with a shake of his head but with laughter writ all over his face. Mr Surya Prakash immediately turned to Mr Chai Zemin and said, " I apologise—I thought that name was valid in a bygone age—now I see that it is still so here. How times seems to stand still for some people!" That is enough," said the President, "No more such jokes." The Indian politely bowed to him and again to Mr Chai Zemin and continued, "Helping oneself to another's property—moveable or immovable—without the person's permission is called Theft. The Americans call it Larceny and depending upon the size of what is stolen they call it Grand Larceny. What China proposes to do by diverting over 30 per cent of the waters of our holy Ganga and about the same percentage of water that flows as the Meghna in Bangladesh can only be turmed Grand Larceny, My Country India has, therefore, forthrightly rejected China's inducements to Bangladesh and us to connive in this clear case of attempted Grand Larceny!" Mr Surya Prakash resumed his seat.

Catching the eye of the President, Mr Chai Zemin stood up again. He was clearly an angry man and his speech reflected that. He said, "China is the country where Yarlung Tsangpo originates. This gives us full rights to use its water in whatever manner we need to, wherever we want to and in whatsoever quantity we want to. That is the law, Mr Indian humorist and there is nothing you can do about it. However, once the course of the river is diverted, there will be some trickle of water flowing in the river bed—you may use that for your needs—we, China permit you to do that." Everyone in the conference hall was shocked at the arrogant tone and words of the Chinese representative. So was the President. At this moment, the other permanent members of the Security Council, one after another, stood up and said, "Our Government has accorded its recognition to the Sovereign Republic of Tibet following the lead of India and Bangladesh and appalled at the treatment of Tibetans by the Chinese. This decision was taken late last night by our respective Governments in view of this meeting and may not yet have been communicated officially to China."

Mr Chai Zemin was shocked. He did not have a single supporter in the Conference Hall! Despite that, he felt it was his duty to stick to his original brief. He said, "This recognition of Tibet is meaningless. We are de facto and as far as we are concerned 'de jure' Government and Tibet is still a province of our great country. So this dramatic announcement is quite irrelevant. In any case, my Government has already sanctioned the SNWD Project and work has been going on for almost a fortnight now."

The Indian representative sought the President's permission to read out a cable from New Delhi, handed to him just when he was entering the Conference Hall and had read only now. On getting the nod, he read out the cable. It was as though he had personally dropped a bomb on Mr Chai Zemin. The gist of the cable was:

- Potala Palace captured without fighting by Tibetan Commando troops who infiltrated into Tibet on foot during the last six days. Potala Palace was liberated and occupied by the Commandos.
- One Special Forces Battalion ex First Battle Group, Free Tibet Army carried out landings at two places close to the two Chinese battalions at 2200 hrs, October 14. They effectively blocked the exit routes of the two Chinese battalions in Area Stadium and Jungzhoi Road, West and have deployed to prevent the Chinese from breaking out of their camps.
- Remainder of the First Battle Group (three Infantry battalions) air landed on Lhasa Gonggar airport which was secured by one battalion. Battle Group less this battalion and Special Forces Battalion moved in locally commandeered transport to Lhasa by midnight to secure Government offices, Bus Station, Railway Station (South of Lhasa river)and arrest/eliminate Chinese (Han) police by 0800 hrs October 15.
- Government of India confirmed that India and Tibet

signed a treaty of Alliance, Cooperation, Friendship and Peace soon after recognition of the Sovereign Democratic Republic of Tibet (SDRT). All military aid including airlift of troops, artillery, ammunition of all types and surface to air missiles have been provided under this Treaty.

- SDRT have declared the air space 50 nautical miles around Lhasa, to be a 'no fly zone ' for all aircraft except Indian civil and military aircraft till further notice.

Mr Surya Prakash said, "The cable is quite 'chatty' and goes on for another couple of pages but what I have covered are the highlights. Would the President like to adjourn this meeting since it appears that China, not being the Lord and Master of Tibet, is no longer the Upper Riparian State for the Yarlung Tsangpo and hence has no 'locus standi' in the matter of SNWD Project, which must wait for a decision of the SDRT when it moves to Lhasa.

Mr Dmitri Pavlov, aware of the other issues that PRC had raised as part of the agenda for this meeting, now addressed Mr Chai Zemin. "Would you like to present before the Council any other complaint against India? On receiving a negative reply from Mr Chai Zemin, the President asked the members of the Council whether they would like to dispose of China's complaint, since it appears that they do not have any 'locus standi' in the matter as Tibet is now not a part of China.

All the members of the Council voted to drop the Chinese complaint except Mr Chai Zemin, who collected his papers and wiping a tear from his eyes, said "Goodbye".

The Council then adjourned.

Chapter-17

The War Starts

Lhasa Sector, October 15, 2100 hrs

The night air landing of the hastily diverted commercial airliners for combat in Lhasa was a surprise to everyone, including the 34th Infantry Division. There was no plan made to attack Lhasa. Even now, the Chinese authorities and even the PLA did not believe that Lhasa had fallen to an attack by Tibetan militia—"By Tibetans, really! You are too funny!" was the reaction of almost everyone in China. They were confident that after grinding Tibet under the heels of their boots for 70 years, there would be no fight left in them. And yet, here was the command from PLA HQ to one of their reserve divisions, 34th Infantry Division, to attack and recapture Lhasa by dawn on October 16.

Hastily a commercial aircraft of China Air and a few large Chinese aircraft were made available at Lanzhou at 1600 hrs for loading. It was almost 2100 hrs when the aircraft pilots were able to spot the runway lights. The first to land was the large transport aircraft ex PLAAF. It carried a Company worth of the Division, the Divisional Reconnaissance and Orders Group and their long range radio set for ground to air /ground communications via which the leading aircraft was to communicate with aircrafts 2, 3, 4, 5, and 6—both to tell them of landing conditions and opposition if any on the airfield and, after unloading, to confirm runway 'clear' for the next aircraft to land.

The pilot of the leading aircraft was surprised to find the runway lit. He made one circuit before he tried to land. Too late he saw a large bulldozer right in the centre of the runway. He could not lift off his heavily loaded aircraft again. The aircraft hit the bulldozer and burst into flames. Explosives inside the aircraft's cargo hold detonated and it was a miracle that two persons, badly burnt, survived the holocaust. And both were stark, raving mad...

A Tibetan detail rushed up to the wreckage in a couple of jeep type vehicles and shot up anyone they thought might be alive. Following them was another bulldozer to roughly clear the runway again.

No 2 aircraft was able to see the lights of the second bulldozer moving away from the runway. The runway lights were still lit. They, however, were able to abort their landing in the nick of time as the wreckage was spotted and the Chinese pilot as well as Battalion Commander who was with him at the time the wreckage was seen were very quick to abort the landing and to order the remaining aircraft to return to base as enemy controlled the airfield.

At dawn on October 16, when the Chinese 34th Infantry Division moved ex Lanzhou by road, they were in no doubt that they would have to fight only after they arrived at Lhasa, tired, hungry and cold. They were too optimistic by about 20 kms as, at that distance, their travails started. At a narrow gorge cut by one of the rivulets that flows into Lhasa river, there was a bridge about 15 metres in span which was found to have been demolished, they had to launch an equipment bridge across the small gap under fire from machine guns skilfully sited to rake the Engineer party along the length and wreak havoc. Among the casualties were 24 engineer personnel and one equipment bridge—dropped into the gorge.

But the PLAAF got in on the act and carried out repeated attacks on suspected hostile positions along the road and closer to Lhasa. On the outskirts of Lhasa one PLAAF aircraft was brought down by an Igla missile. The 'wing man' of the downed pilot turned tail and returned to base with reports of an air defence zone—no less—on the outskirts of Lhasa. He was questioned closely and then grounded.

Jolted by the India-assisted Tibetan rebellion the Central Committee of the Chinese Communist Party (CCCCP) met in a special session at noon on October 16. Commanders-in-Chief of PLA, PLAAF and PLAN were also present. The deliberations could have generated much constructive advice from the members who were present but for the fact that Mr Hong seemed to have decided to convert it into a monologue. He was, indeed, an excellent leader, except for his aversion to being advised or corrected. This session of the CCCCP turned out to be a rambling, ranting monologue. Members had only to play audience and keep their views to themselves or else, share the same fate as that which befell the Late Mr Fang Yamen, ex Railway Minister, on October 12.

Looking somewhat like an angry father chiding his sons who have failed in their examinations, flushed and inclined to make many aggressive gestures, Mr Hong a.k.a the 'Great Helmsman' spoke clearly and to the point.

He said, "Tibet is a collective disgrace for all of you. You, the Party cadres, are the Government's interface with the people—even such undeserving people like the Tibetans. You failed to do that. And now you look up to me and want me to set things right. Let us see if we can approach the whole Tibet issue logically.

First of all, if we control Tibet firmly we shall simultaneously be in control of Yarlung Tsangpo. Then, we can tackle the Indo-Bangladesh objections to the SNWD Project more robustly—no compensation, no appeasement. We wish to do it and are doing it. If they try to prevent us we shall tackle them militarily and bring them to their knees. No other country has a real difficulty with the SNWD Project. As far as Tibet is concerned, it will cease to exist as one unit—whether country or colony or province. It will be carved up into five administrative, centrally controlled prefectures whose boundaries will be worked out by the Interior Ministry. Each of these prefectures will be governed by senior PLA officers known for their ruthlessness and efficiency. They may choose their own assistants and Tibetan speaking PLA personnel as interpreters, translators and so on. No Tibetans—not even a doctor—will be allowed to become part of the governing group. Their task will be to see that Tibetans are fed well enough to work as labour for China; that priests are gradually eliminated and Buddhism is preserved only in the form of a few old paintings, manuscripts and artefacts. Only by finishing off the priesthood and Buddhism can we expect absolutely total obedience from these people. I am not asking you for your agreement with what I have outlined. I am ordering it to be done as I have explained. Interior Ministry will work out all the necessary details within 10 days from now and give me a full presentation on October 26.

We attend next to the recapture of Tibet. Both PLA and PLAAF have put up a miserable performance so far in relation to Tibet. And the two Rifle Battalions stationed in Lhasa and the various Chinese personnel assigned duties at key places like airfield, railway station, Power House and so on have also been miserable failures. Notwithstanding their failure, the matter is not beyond redemption. Lanzhou Military Area Command will be responsible for the recapture of Tibet with its integral forces plus one airborne regiment ex PLA HQ Reserves. They will plan and execute their operations after briefing me fully on October 19. Tibet will be recaptured by dawn on October 26.

We turn next to India. So far India has had things very much their own way. It is the fault of local commanders who allowed themselves to be mesmerised by fire power used by the Indians. From now, PLAAF will earmark sufficient air effort to locate active Indian guns /rockets and destroy them. They shall also ensure that replenishment routes for their ammunition dumps and magazines are systematically attacked and made unusable. As of now, PLAAF will give priority to supporting the PLAA and only thereafter are they to divert some effort to attack enemy air bases which are set well back in relation to the frontline. PLAAF Commander will carry out any other mission that PLAA Commander may order other than the counter-artillery actions.

For the PLAA, I have already spelt out your top priority task—recapture Tibet. To facilitate this task, we need to move the centre of gravity of the fighting to an area about which the Indians are very sensitive—their Arunachal Pradesh (AP) or as it is commonly termed by us South Tibet. You will attack AP with sufficient forces to break through the enemy's defences at least at two points. You will then closely follow the enemy and prevent him from regaining stability and control by successive outflanking movements leading to repeated encirclement of the retreating forces and their annihilation. Take no prisoners; they are a needless burden to guard, feed and accommodate. Your operations in AP will be considered complete when you have reached and firmed in on line Rupa-Itanagar-Pasighat-Teju-Lohit-Walong-Kibitou. This must be achieved by November 7 clearly necessitating a multi-pronged attack.

Apart from your main task I have just spelt out, you will carry out operations against Eastern Ladakh, Sikkim and Bhutan so as to tie down Indian forces in these areas, pose a threat to the narrow Siliguri corridor and prevent reinforcement of the Eastern Sector. Irrespective of the diversionary nature of these attacks, each attack must be pressed home and maximum casualties inflicted on the enemy. Remember, India has built up her strength over the past 20 years or so. Ensure all operations are conducted with overwhelming numerical and fire power superiority and maximum ferocity. There is no need to burden yourself with enemy prisoners. However, for acquisition of battle related or sensitive political information, some prisoners may have to be taken and eventually disposed off when their usefulness has been exhausted.

I shall go over again the time for completion of various tasks:

- Briefing by Lanzhou MAC on Plans—October 19
- Recapture of Tibet—by dawn on October 24
- Presentation by Interior Ministry on Reorganization of Tibet—October 26
- Securing up to the line Rupa-Itanagar-Pasighat-Teju-Lohit-Walong-Kibitou—November 07

So much for PLAA and PLAAF. Now I shall task the PLAN with certain specific tasks which will be carried out by them in addition to what they have been chartered to do in the Operational Directive issued to each PLA segment.

The additional tasks I wish the PLAN to perform are:

- Dominate South China Sea and ensure no Indian, Vietnamese, Taiwanese, South Korean or Japanese ships enter this area. Whereas Indian and Vietnamese ships may be attacked and sunk, others will be firmly blocked and persuaded to go away.
- Dominate India's sea routes through Arabian Sea to West Coast of India in conjunction with Pakistan Navy.
- Prevent any ships—Indian or others—from moving towards India's eastern coast operating from Sri Lankan Port of Hambantota.
- Detail a special force to attack and destroy all three Carrier Battle Groups of Indian Navy.

One special point I would like all PLA segments to note. India considers that the possession of a few primitive nuclear weapons makes them capable of defying our very well developed nuclear armoury. They are relying chiefly on their submarine fleet and missiles of long range to neutralise the threat our nuclear superiority poses to them. I, therefore, want all three segments of the PLA to make all out efforts to destroy their submarine fleet, long range missile bases and any intermediate range weapon locations within or close to the combat zone. Even a single setback to their nuclear delivery system will cause them to come to their senses and end their aggression against us.

That is all, Comrades. I have shown you the way to victory. Follow my directions and we shall triumph. Now go and attend to your duties so that China may win this war as we have won previous wars. Thank you.

Mr Hong walked out briskly towards his car. On the way, he bowed to the statue of the late Chairman Mao Zedong briefly and looking very determined, he got into his car and drove away to his lakeside residence in the old 'Imperial City'.

Chapter-18

Arunachal Pradesh Sector

'A' Coy, 7/8 GR, Midnight, October 16/17

Major Rinchen stopped abruptly near No 3 Platoon 'A' Company. He looked north towards Rima through his infra red binoculars. He could distinctly make out the movement of a large number of the enemy about 800 metres away. He quickly moved to his command bunker and made a call to his Commanding Officer Colonel Bikram Singh and informed him of his observation. "We have also detected the same movement through the BFSR (Battle filed Surveillance radar); I think the Chinese are heading for your Company and also 'B' Company. There has been no shelling so far—perhaps they are doing a 'silent' attack. We shall let them reach Fire line Foxtrot (400 metres) and then let them have it with all our artillery. You may have the privilege of ordering the guns to fire" the CO said. Rinchen was thrilled. He was just about to order some 54 × 155 mm Guns and one 122 mm MBRL (40 Barrelled Rocket Launcher) Battery and one 160 mm Heavy Mortar Battery to fire just ahead of his Company. He gave the order on radio to all concerned on the Divisional Command Net. He asked his Artillery Observer Captain Cheema to give the orders on his net.

Captain Cheema was authorized to call for the fire of the entire Divisional Artillery within range; for anything more, he had to go through the Brigade major of the Artillery brigade. Here is a brief transcript of the first call for Artillery fire made in the Sino-Indian War 2029:

"Captain Cheema: Hello 25 for all stations Uniform 3;
Target U-3979; Scale 3; Fire; Over."

"Brigade Major and all Artillery Command Posts acknowledged the order with a "Roger, Out."

"Precisely two minutes later came a report from the Brigade Major "Shot on Target U-3979, Over."

Cheema and Rinchen, now in the same bunker did not have to put their binoculars up to see what was happening for it seemed as if the entire area occupied by the moving Chinese troops had caught fire and everywhere they were dropping to the ground or running to hide behind rock or some such cover. It was an absolute carnage as the massed fire of the well directed Artillery had inflicted over 60 per cent fatal casualties on the enemy besides wounding the rest. Clearly this wave of the attack had been broken before they could reach the forward wire obstacle.

Badly stung, the Chinese did what, perhaps, they should have done 'ab initio'—called for artillery support for their attack. And now it came—a lethal rain of shells of all calibres, ferocious, deafening in the mountains where the defences were located and very accurately directed. Their effect, however, was nowhere near the lethal effect of the Indian fire—their targets—the Company of Rinchen and his flanking company, commanded by Major Swamy—were in very well constructed concrete bunkers. And yet there were many Indian casualties—due to one bunker in 'A' Company collapsing after repeated 155 mm Shell hits and an Ambulance that was driving up the hill for casualty evacuation in a depth area of 'B' Company. So far 11 casualties had been suffered by 7/8 GR—5 killed and 6 wounded.

The attack continued with the Chinese reserve companies moving towards A and B Companies but covered by their artillery fire. They reached the forward wire and were well on their way into Rinchen's 'A' Company when the DF(SOS), i.e. the closest defensive fire task was ordered to be fired. It came from the 155 mm Regiments supporting 7/8 GR and somewhat in depth of its fire, a regiment of 160mm mortars. The effect of the DF (SOS) was miraculous—almost as if a wiper had wiped the hill-side dry like it does a rain spattered wind screen. The attack broke up by 2.30 AM.

There was a lull before the Chinese renewed their attack on 7/8 GR's positions. During this time an incident occurred which exemplifies the spirit of the infantry soldier. Just inside the forward wire obstacle lay a Chinese soldier whose comrades around him were dead. This soldier, name not known, was hit by the flat end of a large shell splinter and was rendered unconscious. It was a good 15 minutes after all the firing had ceased that he regained consciousness and took stock of the situation. Around him lay his comrades, mission unfulfilled. He decided that he must do his best to complete the mission—'Secure Four Pines Hill'—by himself. He crawled to the body on his right and picked up his light machine gun and four magazines. He then picked up the fallen comrades' two hand grenades and with all this weaponry, the Chinese soldier started moving slowly and very cautiously up the hill side towards 'A' Company. He was a veritable armoury himself; he had his own rifle and three magazines of ammunition, a light machine gun with four filled magazines and four hand grenades. He was, perhaps, 18 years old.

The young warrior closed up to the first bunker, crawled around to its rear and rolled in a hand grenade. All four persons in the bunker were killed. He then lay down on his belly outside the bunker and to a flank and set up the light machine gun. He had targets enough—six men with rifles at the ready were moving in a zigzag manner to their dead comrades' bunker. The LMG spewed bullets at them till all six men lay still. He still had three more magazines left for his LMG. So he fitted a filled new magazine and got up from that position and staggered towards where the six dead had come from. He reached their bunker and lay on its forward side and lay in wait for more reactions from the defenders.

And it came 10 minutes later from two sides. The movement of the Indians was in spurts—one lot moving and the others covering the movement; then interchanging till one lot of six men reached the bunker where the Chinese had taken up a position that was not really good for taking on the on-coming Indians. He shifted about a metre when the movement was spotted. He was fired at by six automatic rifles simultaneously and killed. Cautiously the Indian party approached his body. They knew they had felled one of the bravest of the brave. They took his body to the Regimental Aid Post and told the Medical officer there about the bravery of the dead Chinese soldier. Later the MO said that he had 24 bullets inside him and must have died instantly.

WALONG SECTOR

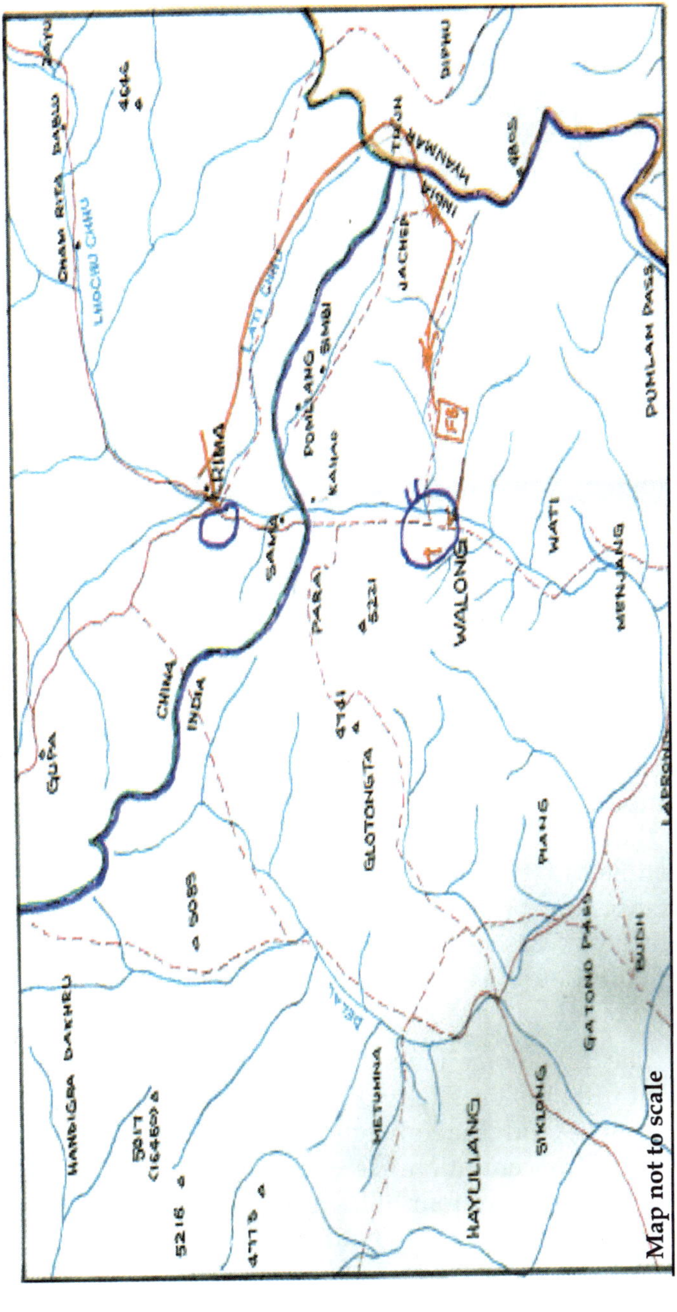

An account of this incident will be found in the War Diary of 7/8 GR. It adds as an Epitaph, "He died for his country, China; and we honour him because his heroism transcended all national boundaries. Bravest of the Brave, it was an honour to have him as our Enemy in War."

The Chinese did not attack 7/8 GR again this night. Perhaps they were licking their wounds or, maybe, they were turning over the badly mauled battalion of the first attack.

Trijunction Sector, October 16/17

Chinese 2nd Infantry Regiment together with 1st Battalion of 102 Engineer Regiment was tasked to make a forced march from Rima to the China-Myanmar-India trijunction and using a steep animal trail leading south from Point 4968 on the watershed for about three kilometres, cross into the Indian side where there is a 'shikari's trail' leading to a point between Road Kibitou-Walong. This route had been reconnoitred a month ago by a small patrol of 2 Infantry Regiment together with a detachment of 102 Engineer Regiment and suitable route markers had been created to help them move smoothly when the time came for the 'real thing' as the Infantry Commander put it. And the time had come. China and India were at war and China's attempt to capture the Kibitou area had been beaten back with heavy casualties. So, the alternative plan by a more difficult route was opted for instead of attacking again and again on the old axis.

The Task Force moved out from general area Rima at about 0100 hrs on Night October 16/17, marched through that night and the following day and arrived at their Forward Concentration Area some eight miles into India, in deep jungle, about four miles from Walong and eight miles from Kibitou. It was at about midnight on October 17/18 when the entire task force had closed up in the Forward concentration Area when it was decided to probe the Walong defences rather than go for Kibitou. Suitable patrols were sent and when they returned, it was with the 'good news' that Walong had only one to two Companies worth of troops holding the Battalion Defended Area—the rest having been sent forward as covering troops or delaying detachments. The Regimental Commander got clearance from the General commanding his Division, for the Walong Defences to be attacked and captured while frontal pressure was maintained on Kibitou. The attack was planned for Night October 18/19, again a silent attack to be supported when required by long range guns only. The H Hour was fixed for 2100 hrs on October 18.

Walong Sector, October 18, 2100 hrs

Faces blackened, everything that could rattle or make a noise cither tightened or jettisoned and each man following the white patch on the back of the one in front, the Task Force moved cautiously towards Walong. There were unexplained stops on two occasions; apparently one direction marker was missing at these two places—probably struck by the foot of a passing animal. So, like so many wraiths, the Chinese Task Force moved on. They reached a pre-selected Dispersal Point from where, on compass bearings, the Company groups into which the column had now split up, moved to their unseen objectives. There was no noise whatever; no one doubted that the men with the compasses were heading for the correct objective. They moved sure-footedly and confidently, trusting their commanders and the column leaders. And they were rewarded.

At 0200 hrs on October 19, one depth locality and two forward localities of the Indian defences at Walong were contacted. The sentry at the light machine gun in the depth platoon had dozed off. The Chinese walked into this Company locality without a shot being fired. The sleeping sentry was put to sleep forever. Now the Company group had to locate the remaining platoons and the enemy Company headquarters.

Noiselessly they organised themselves on the depth Company locality which fell to them without a fight. Machine guns and mortars were deployed and by 0330 hrs, they had firmed in well enough in that locality to make it difficult for the Indians to evict them without a deliberate attack. While one Company was thus busy in defence, the three others were moving cautiously following some telephone cable lying on the ground unburied or homing on to a locality where someone had a bad cough and was making a noise or, listening to someone on a field telephone speaking to the 'B' echelon (administrative elements like cooks, tradesman of various types and so on) asking them to have the tea and breakfast sent to the Companies by 0530 hrs! And so, happy at being so fortuitously guided by the Indians to their localities, the Chinese, with the minimum use of bullets, took over two out of the four localities of the Walong battalion. And they had taken no prisoner having bayoneted to death the few personnel they encountered—perhaps 30 Indians in all. But by now the Battalion HQ and the forward Companies had become aware of the fall of the two rear Company localities and were in a quandary. Should they attack with two companies still holding the forward line? Or, should they reel in the elements that had gone forward as covering troops and delaying detachments? Considering the alternatives, the Battalion Commander ordered containment of the enemy who was lodged in his battalion and blocking the route by which they had sneaked in so that no more forces come in or the 'lodgers' finding the pressure excessive and short of everything from ammunition to food and water, decide to go back the way they came.

The Battalion Commander spoke to the Brigade

Commander, who, with his Rover group was at Kibitou and briefed him about the situation in his area. Brigadier Rampal heard him without comment and after he had completed his account, told him to use one field gun regiment and one 160 mm heavy Mortar battery to make life difficult for the enemy to stay on. He said that he would send back one Company from the delaying position so that he can reinforce his truncated battalion. And then Brigadier Rampal put him at ease by telling him that such things will continue to happen in all wars and therefore, instead of feeling bad or finding someone to blame, one should calmly do what he thinks best for his outfit. "And you are doing just that Vijay—keep up the good work and cheer up your boys too."

Brigadier Rampal's directions were carried out. There was continuous 155 mm gun fire on the depth localities and there were many casualties among the Chinese troops due to the direct hits on two bunkers killing six men and a heavy mortar bomb hitting the Command post bunker leaving him without any means of communication with his troops or with the firm base they had created before they moved to the Indian defences. He could hardly be expected to know that a Company sent back by the Brigadier had tumbled on, by sheer chance, on the cable from the 'firm base' and following it, found it and killed the 11 men who were present there. And then that Company moved along the cable to the depth Company of their own battalion and attacked it from 'the line of march' as it were. The Chinese company, footsore, weary and close to the end of their tether put up a token fight but were killed to a man and the position retaken by the Indians.

The news so cheered the Battalion Commander Colonel Vijay that he ordered all guns allotted to him to concentrate on the remaining enemy lodgements and after a 10 minute bombardment, led the attack with another Company and captured the lost locality. He also took the survivors prisoner—10 men who expected to be shot out of hand now could live under the Indian flag in a PoW camp. The Brigade Commander was informed at 0600 hrs that the situation had been fully restored, that 11 Chinese soldiers had been taken prisoner and our own losses were 16 killed and 28 wounded. Brigadier Rampal said, "Good! Give a shabash to the troops and at the earliest opportunity, send the Chinese to the PoW camp at Hayuliang."

At daybreak on October 19, Indian positions were all intact. The enemy could not break through in the Kibitou-Walong Sector which was his Task.

Let us now turn our attention to Kameng Sector of Arunachal Pradesh.

Kameng Sector, October 16, 1900 hrs

Our surveillance Drones with infra-red sights picked up large Chinese concentrations in general area of Tsona Dzong, Dongka and Karto, all these areas being some 15 to 30 kilometres from the Sino-Indian border. Clearly, these concentrations presaged a major attack on Indian positions in Kameng District of Arunachal Pradesh. Without waiting for the concentrations to break up into task oriented groups, 4 Corps decided to break up their cohesion, ab initio. The fire assault was led by 3 units of extra-long range multi-barrelled rockets, 'Mahakaal' with a range of 90 kilometres. 'Mahakaal' was derived from the Russian GRAD-BM21. There were 18 launchers in a unit and each launcher could fire from all its 12 barrels within 20 seconds. The warhead was of 50 kilogram High Energy Explosive so that one unit could deliver a deadly fire assault of 10.8 tonnes of high energy devastation. The three identified concentrations of Chinese troops were visited simultaneously by one unit each; and the fire assault was carried out five times in all, a colossal 54 tonnes of high energy explosive at each concentration area. The revisit of the Drones to cover the same area they had photographed on the earlier run produced a totally different picture—a scene of huge craters filled with smoke and fire—stretching to about two acres each. There was no sign of human presence or of vehicle/animals of any nature. There was no attack on October 16 or the following day/night. 'Mahakaal' had discouraged further attacks in the Kameng Sector except for long range guns and rocket weapons, which were promptly silenced by own air/gun fire.

Bum La Sector, Night October 17/18

Own Battle Field Surveillance radars all along the Tsona Dzong-Trimo-Lepo and Tsona Dzong-Bum La Axes reported foot columns moving continuously since 2200 hrs or so. Prior to that Chinese Artillery carried out sporadic, harassing fire along the Bum La-Tawang-Nuranang Axis from about 1800 hrs onwards till 2200 hrs. Chinese long range guns also carried out fire against our own Gun positions with some venom and accuracy. We lost two 155 mm Light Field Guns and one ammunition storage bunker, which continued exploding for some time.

By about 0200 hrs, Bum La (East), Tawang (South East) and Nuranang (West and South-West) reported almost simultaneous contact with the enemy. It was painfully clear that despite all our surveillance using drones, radars, observation/listening posts and patrolling of sensitive areas, the Chinese had infiltrated in unknown strength to all these places. He had also succeeded in preventing any vehicular movement forward of Bomdila. The GOC of the Division in whose area all this infiltration had taken place, decided to evict/destroy the infiltrators by a combination of artillery fire and systematically isolating into manageable groups, the enemy and destroying them by physical attacks by up to a Battalion or a Battalion minus one or two Companies size.

By daybreak, Nuranang had been freed of the infiltrators

KAMENG SECTOR

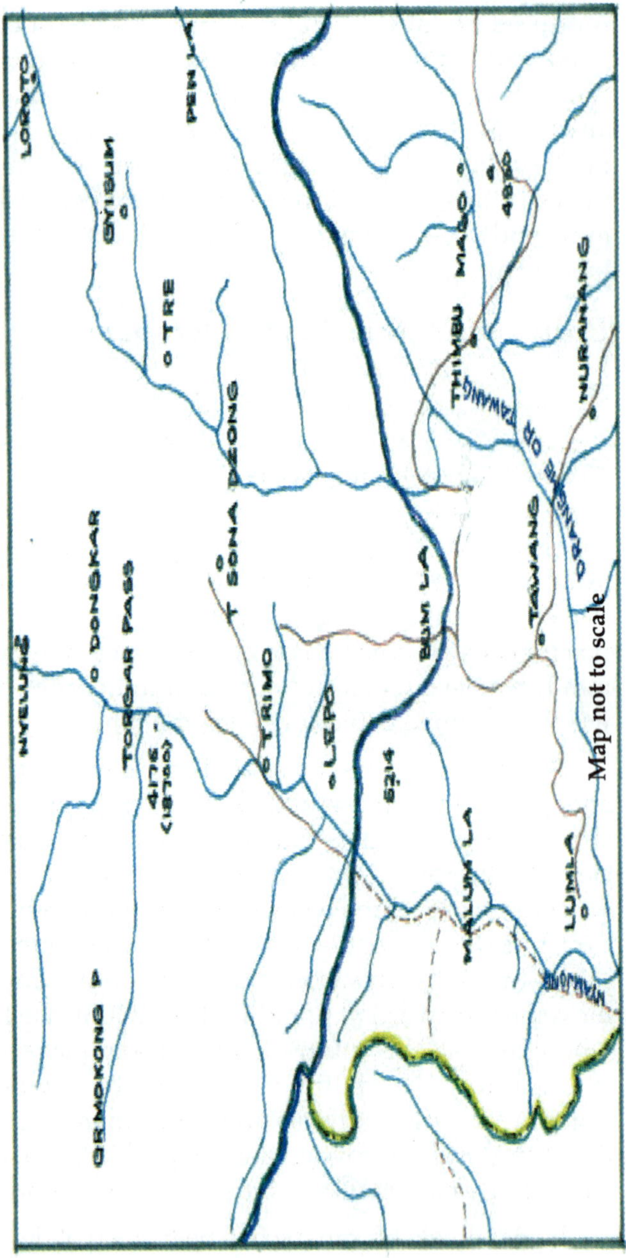

though one small group of about 6 men managed to reach the medium regiment gun position near Nuranang. Here, the gunners fired at point blank range with their guns and soon, neither hide nor hair remained of these brave men. By 4 PM, the last of the infiltrators had been killed in six other actions between Tawang and Nuranang. It was estimated that approximately one Regiment or Regiment minus one Battalion had been employed on the infiltration task.

There was no military activity from the Chinese on the night of October 18. Army Headquarters and Commanders down the line were surprised at the Chinese inaction. Much later after the War, it became known that the Chinese had suffered grievously on October 16 from the bombardment by three Regiments of 'Mahakaal' multi-barrel rocket launchers. The precise numbers of troops killed and wounded will never, perhaps, be made known by the Chinese. However, it is abundantly clear that at 1900 hrs on that fateful day, there were five Chinese Infantry Divisions massed for an attack aimed at capturing Tawang, Bomdila and Rupa. All five divisions appeared to have become casualties in approximately 45 minutes it took for the entire bombardment. Throughout PLA, this news spread like wildfire, demoralising the Chinese on Day 1 of their planned offensive. The only comparison one can find for this kind of a national paralysis and demoralisation was from the infamous A-Bomb attacks on Hiroshima and Nagasaki. The Indians did not use a nuclear weapon and yet the enemy was numbed—indeed, paralysed—into inaction. It was a dream debut for 'Mahakaal' and even the Indians were not expecting the sort of result those 45 minutes produced on the course of the war.

We shall leave Arunachal Pradesh Sector with no more than two remarks:

- The Chinese did not carry out any operation in Arunachal Pradesh after October 18.

- Despite many military 'experts'—both civilian and military goading them to, India refused to settle the status of the 'disputed' areas on the Sino-Indian border in Arunachal Pradesh by offensive action. When pressed for a reply to the question 'Why not?' the Defence Minister Mr Bhim Singh said, "The disputes will settle themselves without fighting." He refused any further comment on the subject.

Chapter-19

India Attacks

Dongkyala Pass, North Sikkim, October 18, 0900 hrs

It was rather windy. Mr Bhim Singh and General Gyani were, fortunately endowed with adequate lung power to be able to discuss the plan that was to be executed that night. General Roy, the Chief of the Army Staff was also present. In fact, it was his plan to get the Defence Minister and CDS over to Sikkim and explain to them the attack plans of the Army in this Sector using the Strike Corps raised in 2020.

After acquainting the visitors with the terrain ahead as far as they could see with powerful binoculars, General Roy got them to move into a large bunker where a map of the area ahead and up to 20 kilometres ahead of Lhasa was displayed. He then briefed them in broad terms about the plan for offensive operations planned for the new Corps.

"Essentially," General Roy said, "The Army plan is to debouch late this evening from exit points I indicated on the ground, at 1800 hrs. Two Brigades of the leading Division, led by two Squadrons of Light Arjun (Abhimanyu) tanks will move at best tank speed towards Khamba Dzong and Traksing Gompa. A Brigade of Infantry will be carried in Armoured Personnel Carriers (APCs) and will follow the tanks about 10 minutes behind the leading tanks. Some Infantry mounted on the tanks themselves will be available to the Squadron Commanders immediately as they are riding on the backs of tanks of the half Squadron following the leaders. All movement is at Tank/APC speed for the flat terrain ahead—say 20 kmph or so."

"Phase 1 Objectives are Khamba Dzong and Traksing Gompa. If there is a fight put up by the Chinese (and I am certain they will), the Combat Group of Tanks with APC-mounted Infantry will attack the opposition from the line of march. However, if the opposition is heavy, Artillery already deployed at start time and stepped up in consonance with the advance at intervals of approximately 45 minutes, will soften the target/targets with an intense 15 minute bombardment with the Divisional Artillery Brigade plus two extra regiments ex the holding formation—108 × 155 mm Light Field Guns. The opposition will be cleared within 60 minutes of contact."

"I visualise that after the holocaust enemy suffered opposite Kameng Sector, he may not be in great heart but, nevertheless, every opposition we meet will be tackled systematically with over-kill preponderance of tanks, APCs, artillery fire and unsettling swiftness. The aim is to get on to Phase 2 latest by first light tomorrow, i.e. by about 0500 hrs."

Phase 2 Objective lie on the Nyang Chhu, 80 kilometres away from Phase 1 Objectives. Nyang Chhu as per the best imagery we have and some Tibetan personnel's previous knowledge, is fordable for tanks and APCs at a few places where the banks are not too close to the vertical. If we find a suitable crossing, we shall cross the Nyang Chhu and reorganise ourself for further advance towards Kongka Dzong-Phase 3 Objective and Lhasa-Phase 4 Objective. Even with opposition at Phase 2 and Phase 3, we plan to be close to Lhasa by first light D plus 4, i.e. by October 22, 0500 hrs. I expect that there may be some resistance offered by the enemy battalion group at Shigatse (on the western flank of our advance) as they have some old pattern half tracks and APCs and may pose a threat to our B vehicle columns which will be about 12 hours behind the leading echelons. As a matter of abundant caution, I have tied up with the IAF to mount a CAP (Combat Air Patrol) to cover the day light parts of the 'B' vehicle movement."

"One final point I would like to make well before D plus 3 and that is the situation in Lhasa. The troops of Independent Tibet Army (Independent Tibetan Army) are still denying the Chinese any approach closer than 10 kilometres from Lhasa. By tomorrow they would have been continuously in battle since October 14. For a newly raised force, they have performed magnificently. Of their four battle groups, the fourth one is yet to receive its baptism of hostile fire. I have been repeatedly requested by their leader in McLeod Ganj to take the fourth Battle Group also as part of our force and give them the pleasure of being in on the relief of Lhasa—which is now in a state of siege. If I have your approval this Battle Group, which is currently at Lachen will be asked to move in transport to be provided by the holding forces and marry up with us by October 20, 1600 hrs wherever we may be at that time. I propose that this Battle Group and one of our combat groups of a tank squadron and one infantry battalion should enter Lhasa together—the Tibetan Battle Group carrying their country's flag blessed by His Holiness, the Dalai Lama. After that, we shall deal with the 'siege' and deal with the Chinese from Lanzhou as I have been informed. If there are any points you wish to raise or any questions you may wish to ask, I shall be happy to do so."

Mr Bhim Singh and General Gyani were highly impressed. They knew that the time plan was optimistic but they felt that with tanks and APCs available in large numbers, it will be possible for the force to maintain or even better the schedule. The Defence Minister approved the entire plan and had only one point to add. He said, "I shall request the Prime Minister to approve the award of an Indian Theatre Honour to the Independent Tibetan Army—'The Liberators of Tibet'." With the CDS too nodding approval, the visitors departed for Lachung (North Sikkim) from where the Indian offensive into the neck of the Chumbi Valley would start.

Ops Room, Lachung, North-East Sikkim, October 18, 1230 hrs

At Lachung they picked up the Corps Commander, Lt General Thambi and were indicated the key landmarks which will be used by him during his briefing. On return, they moved to the underground Operations Room of a formation usually deployed in this Sector. Here, Lt General Thambi, after a round of tea and a snack, started his briefing.

"My plan can best be described as cutting the neck of the Chumbi Salient and then capturing Yatung from the north, i.e. from the rear. The operation will be carried out in three phases as under:

- Phase 1—Capture of Larang and Phari Dzong by a Division less a Brigade each by first light D plus 1.

- Phase 2—One Brigade each to establish blocks at Tang La by last light D plus 1.
- Phase 3—Fresh Division to capture Yatung by first light D plus 3, this to include mopping up of Chinese troops at the watershed by last light D plus 3, assisted by the holding formation.

We have adequate Artillery support—and have tied up with the IAF to give us CAPs by day in the unlikely event that Chinese Air Force is still operating. That is all, Sir. I shall answer any question that you may wish to ask."

Both the Defence Minister and the CDS were very impressed by the 'no frills, to the point' briefing. It was reassuring to meet such clear-headed commanders in the Field. They thanked him profusely and returned from Gangtok to New Delhi.

Daulat Beg Oldi (DBO), October 19, 0700 hrs

Observation post established on top of Trig Height Point 5716 reported the visit of a 4 tonne vehicle based patrol having visited Trig Height at 0600 hrs and having observed the feature through binoculars, leaving on the same route they used for entering the Depsang Plains. Commander 115 Infantry Brigade called immediately for an air strike on Track Trig Heights—Qizil Jilga and Track Trig Height—Track Junction—Chung Tash, South east of Point 4752 and east of Qara Tagh Pass. The target description was 'large enemy wheeled vehicle with 20 soldiers and enemy camps at both target areas.' Since the IAF was using the same map sheet and one of the strike aircraft pilots had visited Trig Heights, he was confident of the air strike coming in as requested. And he was right.

Two IAF aircraft came in from the south and swooping down to about 150 feet above ground level, picked up the moving 'large enemy wheeled vehicle' instantly. The pilot fired two rockets at the vehicle and there was no vehicle or any of its passengers any more. There was only a ball of fire.

The second target near Point 4752 was also spotted—four tents with camouflage nets and about 20 men sunning themselves nearby. The aircraft strafed the men and also shot up the tents. What happened inside the tents is not known, but the men who were strafed would not see a sunrise again.

The aircraft flew over DBO and waggled their wings before flying off to their base.

Commander 115 Infantry Brigade radioed his Divisional Commander (GOC) and said, "It is very lonely here." The GOC understood what the rather peculiar message stood for. It meant "No enemy within 12 kilometres". The GOC gave the order for immediate take off for DBO of 6 × MI 26 type helicopters each carrying a platoon of Infantry—2 Companies worth. These helicopters did four more such trips by 1300 hrs building up the strength at DBO to two Battalions. Around 1330 hrs two AN 32 aircraft landed one by one at DBO and delivered to the troops 6 × 81 mm Mortars, their ammunition, rocket launchers and ammunition and boxes of small arms and machine gun ammunition. The two Battalions felt they were now ready for their assigned tasks.

The tasks assigned to these two Battalion force were to:

- Capture Karakoram Pass and hold it with battalion less two companies.
- Establish a roadblock with the second battalion less two Companies at a suitable site between Shanxi and Qizil Jilga—possible location Tienwendian midway between Shanxi and Qizil Jilga (due east of DBO) and interfere with move of hostile traffic.
- The four Companies (2 ex each battalion) to be used

Daulat Beg Oldi (DBO) Sector

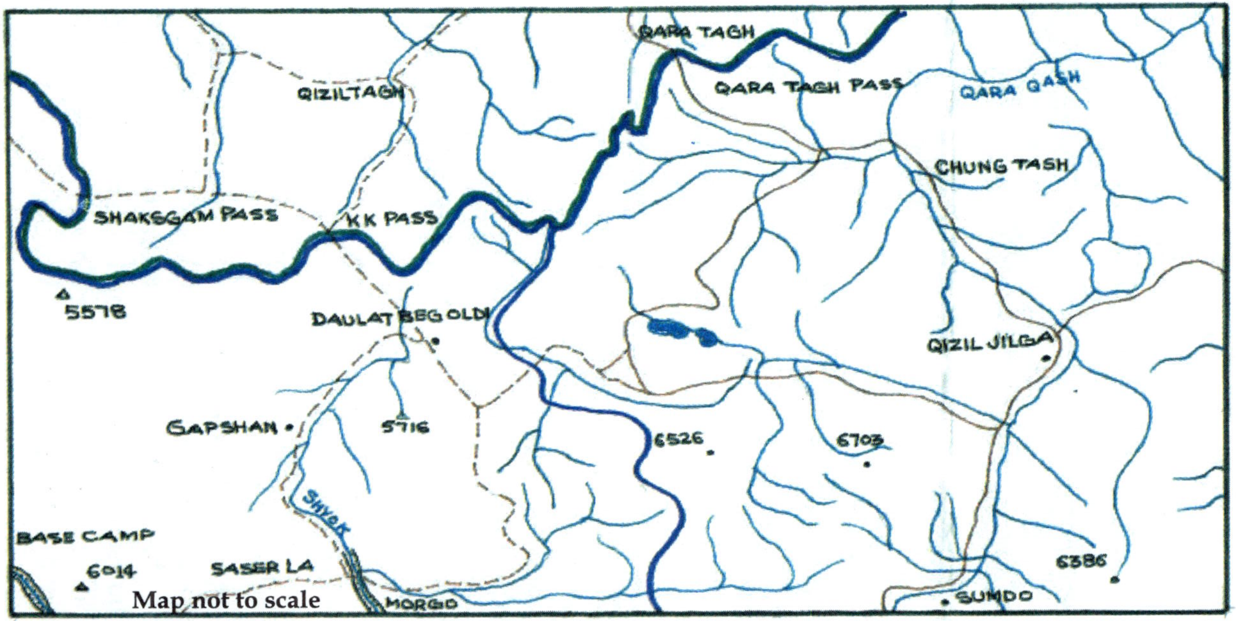

Map not to scale

to attack targets of opportunity based on KK Pass/ Road Block location.

- On instructions, establish contact with Uyghur Freedom Fighters: orders for this, later.

Karakoram Pass, October 19/20, Night

Colonel Prakash, CO 3 Jat was very happy with the way the attack on KK Pass was carried out. Though the Pass was held by a Chinese Border Guarding Force Company, they were unnerved by the first few accurate salvos of mortar fire. They opened fire from all their bunkers/trenches hoping to hit some Indian troops. However, they gave the Jats an excellent idea of where precisely the enemy was. They decided to attack in 'buddy pairs' by stealth, silently walking like wraiths through thickening mist and closer to their objective, crawling silently. On reaching the trench/ bunker, one soldier dropped a grenade inside the trench while the second killed anyone who came out injured but alive. The KK Pass was captured in approximately 20 minutes by little more than a platoon of 3 Jat. 60 enemy lay dead. There was no survivor.

Karakoram Pass, October 20, 0700 hrs

One Jat Company disposed of itself among the bunkers and trenches occupied by the late Chinese troops. They found nearby a convenient gully or gorge and placed all the dead bodies in it before they were noticed by anyone lying about the Pass area. The second Company established two ambushes—one towards Shaksgam Pass due west and the other on the track to Qiziltagh—and lay in wait. The Chinese flag was still flying on the flagpole of the central bunker so that any visiting Chinese would feel secure that they are still in territory controlled by them. At 0830 hrs, two small 1 tonne capacity vehicles were spotted moving towards KK Pass from the direction of Qiziltagh. The look-out posted by the Jats at a point defiladed from the moving vehicles, indicated by pre-arranged hand signal that the vehicles had two men in front and three men in the rear and were clearly carrying cooked food and rations judging by the 'pathilas', sacks and boxes. The ambush party got ready.

The unsuspecting vehicles moving close to each other were now in the 'killing area'. A brisk volley of automatic fire killed the four persons who were in the front of the vehicles. The persons at the rear jumped out to escape the bullets being fired but as they ran to protect themselves on the same route on which they came, they were all shot within the next 30 seconds.

The ambush party detailed two of their men who could drive, to take the two vehicles to DBO. Before the vehicles left, however, they unloaded two pathilas of cooked rice, a dish of potatoes, onions and tofu cubes in a tomato based gravy and about 2 kg of radishes. Also being carried were 2 sacks of raw rice, a smaller sack of lentils and a biggish can of dried fish. There were cartons of tea leaves, sugar and apricot preserves. A good booty thought the Jats who took some of the items but sent the rest with the now Indian driven 1 tonne vehicles.

The Chinese flag was still over the large bunker but the odds were low on anyone else coming their way. So they hauled down the flag and carefully packed it with some sacking, attaching a note saying in Hindi *"Cheen ka Parcham. 3 Jat nay 20 October 2029 ko Karakoram Pass men kabza kiya."*

Tienwendian, Night October 19/20

The two Companies established a strong road block at Tienwendian and had disposed themselves in depth in both the Shanxi and Qizil Jilga directions. It would require a regimental attack to evict them though they were without the usual artillery support and full range of battalion support weapons. They were in position by first light October 20.

The first enemy to attempt bursting through the road block came from the direction of Shanxi. It was a small convoy of three vehicles with fresh troops to replace those killed in the air strike on October 19. They numbered about 40 soldiers from a Transit Camp located about 60 kms away towards Kangshiwar, north east of Shanxi. The troops were vigilant and quite clearly determined to get through to Qizil Jilga, come what may. Unfortunately, their determination was not matched by their strength or the condition of their vehicles.

The warning of the approaching convoy was given by the early warning post by the simple expedient of a short 'tweet' on a whistle and hand signals to indicate the number of vehicles and speed. The convoy was sighted when it was still a kilometre away and grinding its way up the gentle rise towards Tienwendian. After this warning, the Company on the Shanxi side got ready for action. They were made to wait quite a long time as the leading vehicle broke down and was a very reluctant runner after repairs, moving at a crawl and producing copious exhaust fumes. The road block Company waited. These were troops from 1/5 GR and enjoyed 'shikar' of any nature and had a lot of patience.

At last the convoy entered the killing ground. The Company Commander gave the visual signal to his two mortars to fire the 4 rounds each, rapidly and after the fourth round was fired, without a gap, seamlessly the LMGs and the MMG took over. No one had been able to dismount from the vehicles yet. Now, as the automatics firing stopped, three men from the middle vehicle jumped out and charged towards the nearest visible human cluster. It was a brave move and totally useless as their magazines had not been fitted on their rifles! On such small but vital details does human life depend on

AMBUSHES

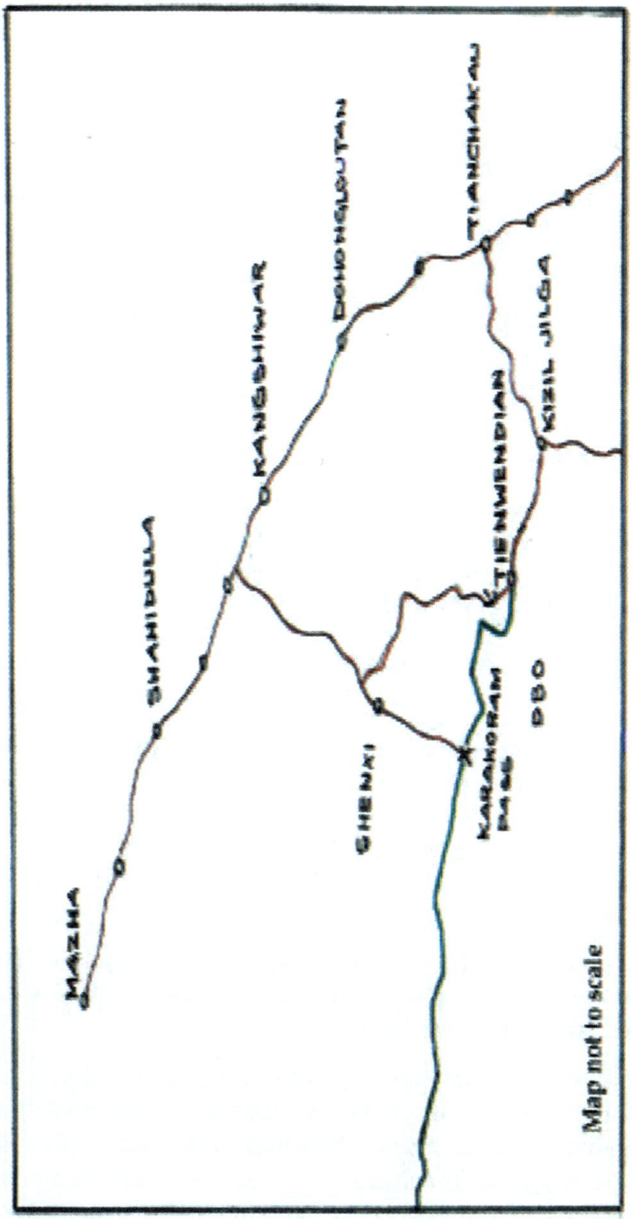
MAZHA
SHAHIDULLA
KANGSHIWAR
DOHONGLOUTAN
SHENXI
TIANCHAKAU
KARAKORAM PASS
TIENWENDIAN
DBO
KIZIL JILGA
Map not to scale

the battlefield. For the men from 1/5 GR, they shot them at a distance of 20 metres and rushing towards them, they made sure that the enemy was dead by checking the bodies out. When they discovered that the enemy had charged at them with weapons that had no magazines on them, they laughed and laughed till the Company Commander called a halt to their merriment. But Gurkhas are irrepressible troops and enjoy a good laugh.

Rummaging through the wrecked vehicles and searching the bodies not too mangled, gave them little of value. Very quickly, the Company Commander got his men to push the vehicles down the hill side where they rolled for about 10 metres and dropped free for almost 400 metres where they found their final resting place.

The Company went back to their action stations. Both the Companies had an uneventful day thereafter and were ordered to build up at Trig Height by night fall as part of their Battalion Defended Area.

Chumar (Eastern Ladakh), October 19-23

Chumar is at the head of an enemy salient and gives him a good launch pad for operations towards Dungti-Chushul or towards Fukche to the east from where Demchok could be conveniently captured. Readers may recall that during the 'stand-off' between India and PRC in 2026, PRC troops seized Demchok which had only a Border Check Post at that time. Since then the recapture of Demchok had been an 'idée fixe' with all Indian troops and Commanders who were posted in this Sector.

The Chinese had upgraded Demchok from being a border check post to being their forward-most defended locality towards India. They had deployed a rifle company with mortars, machine guns and artillery support from Deboche and Tashigong and seemed to have well entrenched themselves in this last Indian border village.

CHUMAR – DEMCHOK SECTOR

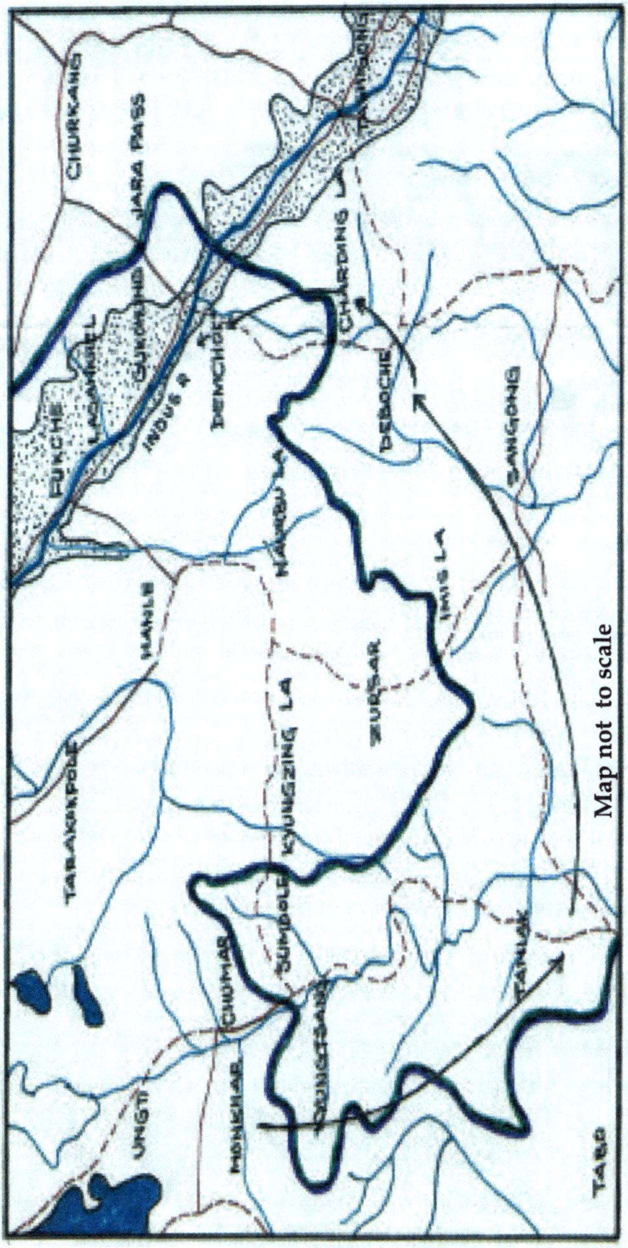

So both sides had their reasons to be wary of each other in this Sector. Now, with an open war going on between PRC and India, our Commander of 43 Infantry Division decided that he would recapture Demchok before the war dwindles to an uneasy ceasefire or peace. He detailed a Paratrooper, now commanding 301 Infantry Brigade, to carry out this task. His orders to Brigadier Lidder were succinct. It read, "Capture the Chumar salient with your Brigade by last light October 22. Thereafter assist 87 Infantry Brigade to capture Demchok on night 23/24 by capturing Charding La by last light October 23. After capture of Demchok your Brigade will be relieved by 1 Jat for further offensive tasks in the Demchok Sector."

Brigadier Lidder, from a family of Paratroopers, was very happy to receive what he called a 'chunky' task. It was tough country and the weather could put one's plans out of gear a little bit—otherwise he did not see any problem in the operation. When asked about the enemy, he said, "He will be killed—that's all about him!"

The troops of 301 Infantry Brigade had become excellent high altitude mountain fighters, thanks to Lidder's very tough and realistic training. And so it was that on the night of October 19, the Brigade entered a Forward Assembly Area around Monkhar. They made their final preparations and by first light on October 20 were ready to receive orders for the actual advance and attack.

The orders were given at a view point near the Monkhar ruins. The plan was for:

- One battalion (1 Sikh) to advance on the western side of the Zanskar Mountains Watershed, capturing Taniak, 16 km away from the Start line by noon on October 21.
- 301 Infantry Brigade less 1 Sikh to capture Kyungtsang and Sumdole by first light October 21.

- Brigade to concentrate in Area Taniak by last light October 21.
- Brigade to recommence advance at 0600 hrs on October 22 along Axis Taniak-Sangong-Deboche-Charding La-Demchok with 1 Sikh leading the advance followed by Brigade R and O Groups, 4 Raj Rif and 5 Grenadiers. Sangong will be secured by 1 Sikh by first light October 23.
- One Company ex 4 Raj Rif will raid and destroy enemy gun position at Deboche by 10 AM on October 23.
- 4 Raj Rif less one Coy to secure Charding La by 1400 hrs on October 23.
- Brigade less 4 Raj Rif to assist 87 Infantry Brigade attack on Demchok from Charding La on night October 23/24—orders will be given for this later.

It was a simple enough plan—drive out the opposition in Chumar salient and having cleared the salient, carry out a deep outflanking movement to attack Demchok from the south, the fire support of the enemy being destroyed en route by a specially earmarked Company. The terrain would be no problem to the Brigade who had been operating in high altitude areas before and achieved very good speeds of movement, cohesion and a certain degree of uncanny ability to overcome obstacles.

The orders seemed to have been overtaken by events. At last light on October 23, the enemy Company stole away in absolute silence for India to repossess Demchok.

Chapter-20

Ceasefire or Prelude to Catastrophe?

Demchok, October 23, 1900 hrs

The sudden melting away of the Chinese troops at Demchok mystified even the battle-hardened troops of 301 Infantry Brigade. They knew that they had done a splendid job of turning the enemy's flank and of destroying their gun position—guns, ammunition and, sadly most of their gunners—basically due to the stocked ammunition having exploded before they could take cover. And yet, the Chinese have never before pulled away in this manner. Brigadier Lidder called GOC 47 Infantry Division on radio and conveyed the success of their assigned mission and the extraordinary behaviour of the Chinese in the last stage—he had checked himself from saying 'the last act in the drama'.

The General replied and said that he had asked the same question of the Corps Commander and both he and the Army Commander who was with him just then after visiting DBO said that they could not explain this strange behaviour of the Chinese. He said a Flash message was just coming in from Army Headquarters and that might give us the reason for what happened not only in Demchok but all over the India-China border. "Something is amiss and we shall soon let you know what Army Headquarters knows" he concluded.

BBC TV News, October 23, 1930 hrs (IST)

"Dispatches have come from our reporters in New Delhi, Leh and Chushul that Chinese troops all along the Sino-Indian Border have been ordered to cease-fire and pull back to their unit HQ areas by 1830 hrs IST. Indian troops who attacked Demchok from the south confirmed that the Chinese Company had pulled out by the time they reached Demchok. The reason for this sudden unilateral cease-fire by the Chinese is not clear. Informed sources say that since the capture of the Tibetan capital Lhasa by elements of the newly raised Independent Tibetan Army, the reverses suffered by them in actions against Tibet and India and above all the enormous number of casualties suffered by them even before they could start their attack in Eastern Arunachal Pradesh, all have combined to make the Communist Party of China lose confidence in the present President, Prime Minister and the Cabinet. Sources hinted at a 'palace coup' but this is pure speculation. We are hopeful that we shall learn, very soon, the motive behind the Chinese cease-fire."

Srinagar (J&K), Joint Operations Centre, October 23, 1945 hrs

Flash message received from Defence Ministry addressed to all service HQ, Command and Corps GOC, CDS and HQ Strategic Forces has been decrypted and is as under:

"Chinese cease-fire declaration now followed by Ultimatum to GOI calling for vacation of Tibet by all Indian and India trained Tibetan separatists within 96 hours ending October 27, 1930 hrs (IST)." (.) Message concludes with: "Failure to comply will lead to active employment of Second Artillery Force (SAF) in response to Indian aggression in Tibet and along the Sino-Indian border (.) cease provocations and comply by October 27, 1939 hrs (IST) or face serious consequences" (.) message ends.

New Delhi, October23. 2000 hrs

Prime Minister's Office, 7 Race Course Road

The impromptu meeting of the Cabinet Committee for Security (CCS) met in the Conference room. All members were present. The Prime Minister briefed them about the contents of the Chinese Ultimatum. He polled the views of his ministers and CDS as to whether they regarded the threat to use nuclear weapons as a ruse to make them comply with their demand – a sort of high level blackmail – or as a serious threat to national Security. All present were inclined to take the message seriously and prepare for a nuclear attack with one or more weapons on military concentrations or any of our nuclear weapon launchers in or close to the combat zone. The general view was that the attacks on population centres will be avoided by the Chinese for fear of our counter-strike. "Does that mean that the deterrent effect of nuclear weapons fails in or close to the combat zone?" asked the Prime Minister.

General Gyani, the Chief of Defence Staff replied, "No. If the Chinese think that they can use a nuclear weapon in or close to the combat zone without fear of our retaliation, they are wrong. My advice to you will always be this—if ever a nuclear weapon is used against any part of India or Indian troops, even on the enemy side of the border, we should react massively and ensure that the offender is reduced to nuclear ash. No, Sir. They must be made to understand that one weapon or ten, sub-kilo tonne or a mega tonne weapon—the Indian reaction will be frighteningly violent."

Others nodded their approval of what the General had said so forcefully. The Prime Minister then asked "In that case, is the threat a bluff?"

General Gyani replied "We will be foolish if we treat the threat as a bluff. We must go in for full scale Nuclear Alert and ready our entire array of counter-strike capability including every ship or submarine at sea. The Chinese should be made aware that we are ready and will not do his bidding."

The Prime Minister then gave the following directions:

- The Nation be kept informed of the situation—fully.
- We agitate the matter in the UNSC and enlist all our powerful friends in the international community to tell China not to invite disaster.
- Ensure that all our first and second strike assets are readied for instant reaction.
- Our entire range of electronic warfare assets must swing into action immediately.
- A variety of platforms—on land, sea, in the air and from space to commence massive electronic jamming of all known or suspected Second Artillery Force communication networks.

- Electro Magnetic Pulse (EMP) attacks be carried out on Beijing, Shanghai, Canton, Chengdu, Hong Kong and the location of the Chinese National Command Post and its alternative locations (if known), the idea being that the Chinese leadership must be prevented from meaningfully controlling their forces.
- Based on what happens at the UNSC Emergency Session, I shall give orders about moving into nuclear shelters, if unavoidable. Till then, no move underground.

The meeting of the CCS ended by 2100 hrs and its members went off to their respective offices.

Meanwhile, totally oblivious of the momentous going-on elsewhere, an Indian merchant man moving from Aden to Kochi Harbour, spotted a flotilla of four ships at a distance of 3 nautical miles. The ship, *MV Maurya* moved on its course without alarming the flotilla which must have picked up his ship on radar as well as visually. Perhaps because they were all pre-occupied with something more momentous, they failed to note the *Maurya* disappearing towards Kochi. If they had, there would have been a different tale to tell.

Nine Degree Channel (Minicoy)

October 23, 2115 hrs

The Captain of *MV Maurya,* Captain Bhaskaran was formerly in the Indian Navy. He found his way up the promotion ladder blocked and retired prematurely. He was lucky to be employed almost immediately by a private shipping company and had become Captain of his own ship just a year ago. He knew the importance of what he had seen. So, transiting through the channel, he radioed a message to the Harbour Master, Kochi for immediate passage to the Flag Officer Commanding, Southern Naval Command. The message reached Vice Admiral Jacob within 10 minutes. It read "Message received from Captain of *MV Maurya* ex IN, Retd Lt Comdr Bhaskaran. He has reported a flotilla of four foreign naval ships, probably Chinese, at 61 degrees east-10 degrees North at 2045 hrs. Flotilla consisted of one large ship—possibly Destroyer and three smaller ships—possibly frigates. Happy hunting!"

The Flag Officer Commanding, Southern Naval Command spoke immediately to his counterpart in Western Naval Command and the two of them arranged to check out the flotilla. One Submarine and a flotilla of a Destroyer and two frigates was in the general area of Maldives. They were directed to intercept the unknown ships and, if they turned out to be Chinese, to sink them. The submarine was moved out first. The flotilla was reported to have veered southward towards Lakshadweep so that the presence of our ships in the area of their destination was fortunate. The Submarine, moving fairly quickly at periscope depth, sighted the four ships closing on to the Indian island of Lakshadweep and positioning themselves at about 1000 metres, opened fire on the northernmost island. They missed it by a fair margin. But the Submarine lurking silently at periscope depth, drew a careful bead on the Destroyer and fired two torpedoes at it. Even as the torpedoed were running towards their target, the Indian ships opened fire on the enemy flotilla. The torpedoes scored hits. So did the next two torpedoes fired at the same ship. The Destroyer sank silently after rolling over on its side. It was a big kill for the submarine—IN's first against China in this War. The combined shelling of the Indian flotilla caused great confusion among the remaining three ships of the Chinese. Two of them were hit by the Destroyer's guns while the Indian frigates added to the enemy's casualty list by landing quite a number of rounds on the decks. It was then that a shell fired by the Destroyer, providentially hit a magazine which exploded. The frigate was blown into two pieces and sank within two minutes.

The remaining frigates tried to get away by moving off at high speed towards Maldives but failed to make good their escape. They were sunk after an hour long battle with the trio of Indian ships. Thus ended the first naval battle of the Sino-Indian War of 2029. The result: enemy lost one Destroyer and three frigates. Own surface ships received a number of hits but were not seriously damaged. The submarine came through with a Destroyer kill and no damage.

At dawn, Maritime Reconnaissance aircraft spotted some survivors and vectored our ships on to them. 14 PLAN personnel were rescued and taken by the Indian flotilla to Mumbai to be confined in a Prisoners of War Camp opened recently on the outskirts of the great city.

New Delhi—Preparing for War, October 24, 1000 hrs

Indian Navy Deployment

News of the Naval battle in the Nine Degree Channel area of the Arabian Sea/Indian Ocean was received with glee by everyone. Mr Bhim Singh sent a congratulatory message reading "Shabash! Up the Navy." During the night, confirmation had also been received about the location of our ICBM equipped submarines and their security arrangements. Note was also taken of our Carrier Battle Groups deployed so as to cover the seas/oceans girdling all of South Asia, South and East China Seas and the Eastern Pacific Ocean.

Electronic Warfare

Own Electronic Warfare was proceeding in a systematic manner. A large number of radio nets of Second Artillery Force units had been acquired and more are likely to be acquired. The notional communications diagrams drawn up by own Electronic Warfare experts were rather well thought out and corresponded closely to the actuals being acquired. When the time comes to jam them, they were confident that their command net, alternative command net and a third they termed the Second Stand by Command Net had all been acquired and could be jammed at will. Most units of the SAF were also working on net radio and could be jammed easily. However, a glaring lacuna was noticed when we discovered that fibre-optic connections were difficult to locate and destroy. The drill for this was hastily worked out at the concerned Signals unit.

EMP

The preparations for 'frying' the key electronics based command and control circuits of the Chinese by massive electro-magnetic pulse attacks were well under way. Confidence level was very high that when the crucial moments arrive they will be without communications—everything electronic—even down to a cardiac pacemaker—will be 'fried', i.e. their innards will receive such a high voltage surge that they will be crippled—damaged beyond repair/redemption. Of course, the timing must be exactly right for the EMP attack to be optimally effective.

Intelligence Activities

The R and AW was in full strength. Its agents were already at appropriate places. 'Sleepers' were woken up and activated on special tasks. 'Friendly' agencies from other countries—USA, UK, Russia and some others offered additional intelligence cover and a double check on crucial intelligence product generated by R&AW. All told, 'Intelligence' was ready for the 'Big Fight'.

7 RCR, October 24, 1830 hrs (IST)

Prime Minister Jagannath Das issued a carefully worded rejoinder to Beijing's ultimatum—one which conveyed quiet confidence, the strong backing of a large number of friendly countries and a desire to convey that issuing the Ultimatum as China did was not in China's interests. This is what our Prime Minister's message to the Chinese read:

"You have considered it fit to subject India to the threat of nuclear attack in defence of your imperialist policy on Tibet, Eastern Turkestan and Southern Mongolia.

We wish to remind you that we too are a significant nuclear power and are backed by the whole world with the solitary exception of your only friend and protégé People's Democratic Republic of Korea.

Any hostile action taken by you against us anywhere in the Sovereign Democratic Republic of Tibet or on our own soil in India will be met with unimaginably vigorous retaliation that may cost your country heavily.

You are advised to withdraw your ultimatum as we do not wish to embarrass you by rejecting it before the whole world."

Beijing, October 25, 0700 hrs

The atmosphere in the Underground Bunker, some 70 km from Beijing was oppressively tense. The President Mr Hong was walking to and fro in his spacious office bunker. He seemed very excited about something and was chuckling to himself from time to time. The Indian Prime Minister's response to the ultimatum had not yet been put up to him. No wonder Mr Hong was chuckling to himself. He might be saying to himself, "The Indians must be frozen with terror which even talk of a nuclear war inspired." In a few minutes, he would feel quite differently....

The Premier Mr Lung was ushered into his bunker. He looked as if he had not slept all night. He held out a Red folder to the President who waved him to a seat. Before he could say anything at all, Mr Hong opened the folder and started reading the Indian response. His expression changed in a remarkable manner. You could read the changes from the initial disbelief, to one of shock as the purport of the message reached his brain; the anger at the audacity of the Indian followed by an expression of bewilderment. "What am I to do now? Where have I gone wrong?" The President's face reflected the surge of questions that invaded his mind. And then the enormity of what he had tried and how he had failed struck him so clearly that his face collapsed from the cherubic to the ravaged face of a person who has been caught red handed, doing something heinous. He stood up but his legs gave way and he fell back in his chair. His face ashen, he said, "Lung, can I have a cup of tea, please?"

Mr Lung hastened to procure the green tea the President favoured in a few minutes. Mr Hong was able to fortify himself with that life giving fluid. He got a grip on himself, smiled (actually it was like a grimace) and asked Mr Lung, "Has there been any further reaction?"

The Premier said, "Yes, Sir. And every one of them is asking us to withdraw the Ultimatum."

Mr Hong nodded. He said, "I see. Call all our major leaders who are in this Command Bunker to meet in one hour—say, at 0830 hrs, for discussion of the situation that has arisen."

Mr Lung said, "The Presidents of the USA and France and the Prime Ministers of Russia and the UK have been trying to speak to you since late last night. Would you like to speak to them before the meeting? If so, we could have the meeting a bit later."

The President shook his head. "I shall speak to these

dignitaries now and still be able to attend the meeting at 0830 hrs. It is no good postponing what has to be done—however unpleasant it may be. Okay?" Mr Lung was happy to note that the President had got a grip on himself and was now much like what he used to be before the SNWD Project was activated. He nodded and went to the next bunker to give instructions for the President's calls to be put through to him one by one. He then went to the office room to give instructions about the conference the President wanted to hold.

The President had another cup of green tea and picked up the receiver for the American President's call. The American President—believe it or not, named 'Bunker'—sounded as if he was right next door. The American said "Good Evening, Mr Hong or rather Good Morning to you. I would hate to put it this way but we Bunkers shoot straight from the hip. If you want to have a good morning, withdraw that ultimatum you have served on India. I mean, recall it, tear it up, throw it away. Do you know what will happen if you do not? Let me tell you, your crazy ultimatum would have started a Nuclear War and finished off the World. Am I making sense?"

Mr Hong cut in and said in a rather suave polished manner "Mr Bunker, you used so many words that I was wondering what you were trying to say! Correct me if I have got you wrong but what I gathered from your talk was that you want me to withdraw the ultimatum. Right?"

Mr Bunker, who was at a cocktail party at the White House said, "That is exactly it. So will you do it—I mean will you withdraw your ultimatum?"

"Yes, Mr Bunker, we shall certainly consider it" said Mr Hong. "I am meeting my colleagues and will take an appropriate decision in the matter."

"Good, do consider. If the decision is not to the liking of the rest of the World, you may regret it—regret that one action of yours has turned China into a nuclear waste land. So go ahead and do the right thing. Good luck and good bye Mr Hong." Mr Bunker rang off.

At two minutes interval between calls, Mr Hong spoke to the leaders of France, Russia and the UK. Their message was essentially the same as Mr Bunker's—except that they sounded like real life leaders of important countries and were polite; but they too made the same 'suggestion' but stressed the urgent requirement of withdrawing the ultimatum, the British Prime Minister going so far as to say, "Time is very important in this matter. You see, there is a possibility that the other side may try to forestall you and get in their nuclear strike on you, first! So, Mr Hong, I am sure you will do whatever is in the interest of all of us. Thank you for listening. Bye."

Mr Hong looked at his wrist watch. Half an hour to go for the meeting. He ordered breakfast to be served to him in his office and while waiting for it, he recalled, from his youth days spent in England, a stanza from Robert Burns' poem 'To a Mouse'. "The best laid schemes o' Mice an' Men,/Gang aft agley/An' lea'e us nought but grief an' pain,/For promis'd joy!"

Mr Hong sadly shook his head. Grief and pain certainly have been achieved but there is no promise of joy. Moodily, he skewered a pickled apricot and waited for Mr Lung to fetch him for the Meeting.

Chapter-21

The President Decides

Beijing, October 25, 0830 hrs

The top leaders of the Government and the Chiefs of all branches of the PLA had gathered together in the brightly lit Conference Hall. The atmosphere was almost funereal. All of them knew about the loss of Lhasa and the recognition of Tibet as a free country by the leading nations of the world. They knew too of the terrible fate of Chinese troops opposite the Kameng sector—five divisions being totally written off by the Indians using multi-barrel long range rocket launchers with enhanced energy war heads. It made one sick to even think of nearly 50 thousand soldiers being killed in less than 45 minutes from over 50 kms away. The first impression that was conveyed to the rest of the country was that the weapon was probably a mini nuclear bomb and that India had tried to hide its 'first use' by firing the multi-barrel rocket launchers. Everyone present felt a sense of outrage against India.

Mr Hong entered at 0830 hrs and bowed to the members present. He then took the mike and said, "Comrades, you are well aware of the Ultimatum we have issued to India. It expires at 1930 hrs on October 27. I intended that if the ceasefire is broken before that time, as indeed it has, we should teach the Indians a lesson. Already on October 23, at about midnight, the ceasefire was violated by Indian naval ships and a submarine in the area of the Maldives. In a sudden attack by one or more submarines, four PLAN ships—a Destroyer and three frigates have been sunk. There were only 14 survivors and they are now Prisoners of War in India. I consider the Indian action despicable and cowardly and needs to be punished."

Mr Lung stood up and asked Mr Hong as to how he came by this information. Mr Hong replied, "A Pakistani corvette was able to see the whole wretched action and informed their Naval HQ. The Pak President gave me this information just now on telephone."

Mr Lung became very agitated. "The Indians have certainly cheated us," he said. "We should call off the ceasefire and let the Ultimatum stand till we have punished the Indians sufficiently. But Sir, what about the heads of the USA, France, Russia and the UK who tried to pressurise you to withdraw the ultimatum immediately? Did they not know about this dastardly attack on the PLAN ships? They must have known and yet, have kept quiet about it! Their pleadings to you, therefore, may have to be re-evaluated."

Mr Hong smiled for the first time since he entered

the Conference Hall. He said, "I agree entirely with what you have said. India has violated the ceasefire and needs punishment. However, if the ultimatum expires, we shall then be honour bound to execute nuclear attacks against the enemy and face his second strike in response. My young friend, war is not a game of 'Ping Pong'. In this terrible business the odds are stacked against us. But let us ask the Commander of our Second Artillery Force what he can achieve with different levels of nuclear strike by us and what might the enemy and other countries do. So, General Lee, you tell us this: We hit India—India hits us back—USA, France, Russia and the UK also hit us because they have specifically said so to me. What is the chance of our emerging from this war with Honour?"

General Lee, who had a reputation for intellectual integrity of the highest order and who never minced his words said, "Mr President, I am glad you have asked me this question and I shall reply with absolute frankness. If we fire even one nuclear weapon against the Indians, they will, of course, reply with a nuclear weapon. However, having studied their nuclear doctrine, they will retaliate massively and with 'no holds barred' as I heard one of their National Security Advisors say when I met him in South India when I had gone there for attending an Aviation Expo in which we were also participating. When I probed him further, he said 'if anyone fires one nuclear weapon against us—even if it is a small yield weapon—say like 1 kilo tonne, we shall respond to it as if the other party had fired off his entire stockpile of nuclear weapons. And rest assured that not much will survive in the 'first strike country'—perhaps a few radioactive vultures picking at the bodies of the nuclear dead before they too die of the radiation. No Sir, it was not 'party talk'. It was a sober discussion and the answer he gave left me in no doubt whatever that if you order me to strike with nuclear weapons, I shall, but I guarantee you that China will not emerge after the counter strike. I hope, Sir, I have been clear in my reply."

There was stunned silence in the Conference Hall. Everyone seemed to have frozen into a silence so eloquent that it seemed to say 'No nuclear weapon, we would like China to live on'! And yet, no one spoke.

Mr Hong, who a few minutes ago, was for revenge against the Indians, seemed to have turned rather pale with the horror of what his Commander Lee had described so morbidly well. And being himself a very honest man he said to General Lee, "General, if India retaliates with every nuclear weapon it possesses, will the other nuclear powers 'nuke' us or India?"

The General said, "Sir, it makes no difference at all because when we are attacked with a nuclear weapon, People's Republic of Korea (North Korea) would also have been attacked as they are our ally and may have responded to the Indian counter strike; my reading is that they too would be engaged in the counter strike. Further, even if the other nuclear powers do not join in the Sino-Indian nuclear war, the all-pervasive, universal effect of so many nuclear weapons bursting in the Earth's atmosphere will wreak havoc with all humanity and spread such pollution—a radioactive and hyper-toxic miasma that no living creature can survive. Sir that will be the end of the human race—not perhaps in a day or two but over a period of indeterminate length of continuous, awful suffering—but in the end the human race will cease to exist."

Mr Hong spoke sombrely: We were not entirely ignorant of the consequence of a nuclear war but what General Lee has told us suggests to me that at least I, your President, have much to learn! In order that all of us benefit from having heard his very frank and forthright talk on the possible effects of a nuclear war, I would like you to spend the next 30 minutes in discussing the subject amongst yourself. After 30 minutes, resume your seats. I shall then call upon four members in each row to share their views on these questions:

- First: Should we withdraw the Ultimatum despite the ceasefire violation against PLAN?
- Second: Should we withdraw the Ultimatum but retaliate against India in a limited conventional operation?
- Third: Should we refuse to withdraw the Ultimatum and carry out a 'token' first strike with a sub-kilo tonne nuclear weapon in the battle zone?
- Fourth: Should we refuse to withdraw the Ultimatum and carry out a massive first strike all over India and reduce India to a nuclear wasteland?

You may now form small groups of your choice and arrive at answers for each one of these. The next 30 minutes are all yours. Thank you." Mr Hong, Mr Lung, General Lee and Mr Chai Zemin (back from the UNSC) formed a small group too and discussed the answers to Mr Hong's four questions. Mr Hong was with them in person, but his heart had sped off to the watery grave where 800 brave PLAN personnel had lost their lives less than a day ago…

Everywhere in the Conference Hall, small groups of four or five had formed and were discussing their answers to Mr Hong's four questions. It was a serious business—a matter of life and death for not just China or India but for the whole world. So the discussions were quite often forceful, sometimes even sarcastic and occasionally even vitriolic when someone felt his views had been laughed at or disparagingly treated. Yet, as the minutes ticked away, a kind of expectant calm seemed to be replacing the agitation and heat of discussion. People were shaking hands with their 'groupies' and resuming their seats. At the end of 30 minutes, Mr Hong and his group entered. Mr Hong went to the microphone and asked the House, "Are you ready?"

"Yes!" Came the resounding reply. Mr Hong then asked four people from each of the 15 rows for their answers to the four questions. Mr Lung recorded what the responses were. It was time-consuming but very orderly like most Chinese group activities are. Surely time spent on considering the answers to the four questions, was well spent—the lives of over 6 Billion human beings depended on it. It took over two hours for the answers to emerge. Once Mr Lung had shown his record of answers to the questions and his analysis of the views that prevailed in the end, Mr Hong once again addressed the gathering.

Mr Hong said "60 answers to each of the four questions have been thrown up. Mr Lung has stated that out of the 300 persons present in this Hall, the answers of the 60 groups as classified emerges as follows:

- First Question—Yes: 260; No: 40
- Second Question—Yes: 30; No: 270
- Third Question—Yes: 10; No: 290
- Fourth Question—Yes: 0; No: 300

Comrades! I have now read your pulse. What you feel, all of China feels. I shall go by what 260 of you have said but before the Sun is any higher in the sky, a very strong protest will be lodged against India in the UN Security Council for last night's ceasefire violation. We shall demand from India a clear apology and an undertaking against any repetition before we can reconsider the question of withdrawing our Ultimatum. We shall ask for the reply within the next 24 hours. The consequences of their defaulting on the time allowed to them may result in a great tragedy for the whole world. I thank you Mr Lung for a quick and clear analysis of views. And to all my Comrades here, thank you."

The meeting adjourned.

Chapter-22

China Complains to the UNSC

UN Headquarters, New York, October 25, 1000 hrs

True to his word to the 300 who attended the morning meeting in Beijing, President Hong sent the following EMERGENCY Message to the UN Secretary General Mr Robert Starr:

- Firstly (.) A number of Indian Navy ships and at least one submarine ambushed and destroyed a Chinese Naval flotilla of one Destroyer and three frigates in the general area of the Maldives at about midnight October 23/24 (.) only 14 PLAN personnel survived this dastardly attack (.) they are now in a PoW camp near Mumbai (.)
- Secondly (.) In consonance with our ceasefire declaration of October 23, our forces were restrained from retaliating (.) this, however, has evoked highly adverse reactions from the people of China (.) there is pressure building up to retaliate with powerful hypersonic cruise missiles with a variety of warheads against sensitive Indian civilian and military targets (.) PRC Government apprehends that unless India makes immediate amends for the ceasefire violation and attack on our ships, the ceasefire may entirely break down and the ultimatum expiry time being advanced from October 27, 1930 hrs to October 26 1800 hrs (.) the onus of such a grim prospect will lie squarely on India (.)
- Thirdly (.) In order to avoid the calamitous transformation of ceasefire into a full-scale nuclear war, certain steps spelt out in fourthly below must be taken by India as the violator of the now fractured ceasefire by October 26, 1000 hrs.
- Fourthly (.) Steps to be taken by India by October 26, 1000 hrs follow:

  alpha (.) express deep anguish and regret for unfortunate violation of ceasefire leading to naval encounter between IN and PLAN at about midnight October 23/24 (.) loss of life of all except 14 PLAN sailors, now in Indian custody, to be deeply regretted (.)

  bravo (.) India to undertake to scrupulously abide by

the ceasefire declared by the People's Republic of China and ensure no lapse of any nature occurs again.

- Fifthly (.) The question of withdrawal of our ultimatum to India scheduled to expire at 1930 hrs on October 27 will be considered after confirmation that actions as required vide para fourthly have been taken by India (.)
- Sixthly (.) This entire message may be copied at UN HQ to reps of all members of the Security Council as now constituted (.)
message ends.

UN Headquarters, October 25, 1200 hrs

Mr Robert Starr, Secretary General was taken aback at the contents of the PRC message demanding India's apology and undertaking to scrupulously observe the ceasefire in force. While the time limit for completed action as given by PRC was only one day, Mr Starr was rather doubtful about the Indians sticking to the time limit. He rang up India's Permanent Representative at the UN, Mr Arun K Roy and asked him to come over to his office.

On his arrival Mr Starr said, "AK, I know from previous experience that Indian politicians are very thorough and take any decision only after 'deep and mature consideration'. This time around, could you persuade them to step on it and send their reply within the next 5-6 hours? Otherwise, we may land in a very deep hole and may be able to consider nothing except the prospect of a nuclear war."

Arun K Roy replied, "I have already spoken to the Foreign Minister and also the Prime Minister as he had recently consulted me on an India-China issue. Both of them assured me that the Indian reply will be in your hands and in Beijing by about 1800 hrs today. They told me that there was no difficulty in sending the message Beijing drafted in their 'Fourthly' as the whole ghastly incident took place because the flotilla did not get the message about the ceasefire, ultimatum and all that! I wonder who is responsible for this foul-up but no matter how it happened, I am told on authority that the encounter between the two flotillas—ours and China's—was due to a communication failure on our side. Sad, but true."

Mr Starr asked, "Did your Foreign Minister or the PM say anything about sending copies of the Chinese demand to all the current UNSC members?"

Arun K Roy said, "Yes Sir. No problem on that. The PM actually said that it will be good for everyone to know that the mistake was ours and that the Chinese have acted in a fair and reasonable manner—except, of course, for their pre-occupation with Hitlerian ideas like Ultimatum and so on."

Mr Starr smiled and said, "Nice talking to you, AK. Be seeing you after the Indian reply comes in. Bye then."

AK walked back to his fairly small office. He had not had a wink of sleep for the past 48 hours. 'And people say the UN posting is a 'cushy' one!'—this was his thought as he sat down on a sofa-seat in his office and fell asleep instantly, sitting.

The incessant ringing of the telephone woke him up. He noted that it was already 1700 hrs. He walked to his Secretary's office and asked, "has India replied?" The Secretary smiled and said, "Yes Sir. Even their wording is the same as that of the Chinese. UN has confirmed that China too has got the message."

Beijing, October 25, 1900 hrs

The mood in the Presidential Bunker was considerably lighter than it was that morning. The Indian reply had been received and their own demands had been fully met. Honour thus satisfied, Mr Hong breathed easier and from time to time said to himself, "We may have done badly in the war so far but we still have a good chance of winning a Peace with Honour." He was deep in meditation with this thought 'Peace with Honour' in his mind when his meditation was disturbed by the telephone ringing. His Secretary informed him that the UN Secretary General Mr Robert Starr was on the line and would he, the President take this call? "Certainly, but certainly, please put me through" the President said.

"Good Evening Mr President," Starr's voice was clear and confidently loud. "Thank you for taking this call for I know you must have been very busy."

Mr Starr ascertained from the President his reaction to the Indian reply—whether he wanted to pursue the matter of the ceasefire violation any further. Mr Hong said, "The Indian reply was very satisfactory." Continuing, he remarked, "Now that incident is over and done with. What I would like to discuss with you is whether you are prepared to call a special meeting of the UNSC to reconstruct a more durable peace."

Mr Starr concealed his astonishment at this initiative on Mr Hong's part. He replied cautiously, "Certainly Mr President, whenever you wish me to, I shall do so. However, we are still in a 'ceasefire' mode and your 'Ultimatum' is still poised like the proverbial 'Sword of Damocles' over the head of everyone in the World. Do you, Mr President, consider that if these two de-stabilising factors were removed, the meeting you desire me to call will yield quicker and more positive results?"

"That is a very fair question. Ideally, the UNSC meeting will be productive if the parties attending have a reasonable degree of mutual trust and no troops are on foreign soil.

The same applies to the Ultimatum: unless the aggression committed by India against us is vacated, there is no question of mutual trust nor, and I would like to stress this, no withdrawal of the ultimatum. Obviously, no UNSC meeting under those circumstances will be productive. Indian troops must vacate Chinese territory soonest possible. I think a week will be more than enough for this purpose. China shall withdraw the ultimatum when the Indian troops withdrawal is completed in a maximum of 7 days or earlier. We shall, till the withdrawal is completed, rely on the Ultimatum to prevent any breach of trust by India. If you are in agreement with my formulation, you may consider calling for the UNSC meeting on November 4."

"Thank you, Mr President, for your clear enunciation of China's position. I shall speak to the Indian Prime Minister also and inform you what transpires between us. We could then finalise the date for the UNSC meeting."

Mr Starr continued, "May I ask you what your views are about Tibet declaring herself independent and the recognition of the Tibetan Republic by all the great powers and some 25 countries more? I ask this question as Tibet has applied formally to be granted membership of the UNO."

President Hong rubbed his stubbled cheek meditatively before replying to this sensitive question. "Let me have a cup of Green Tea first; I find it soothes the nerves and stimulates the grey cells of the brain."

Mr Starr did not quite know how to react to this. Weakly he asked Mr Hong, "I hope, Mr President, I have not offended you by broaching this subject now."

"Not at all. Just let me have a few sips of the Green elixir and you can ask me anything you like."

After a few sips of his favourite potion, Mr Hong continued in an easy, relaxed manner. "Mr Starr, in China we play a board game like Chess. It is called 'Wei Chi'. In Chess, one tries to checkmate the opposing King; in Wei Chi, to win, the player has to achieve a strategically advantageous position vis-à-vis his opponent. If strategic 'edge', however small, is secured by one player, he is the winner. In much the same way, the Tibetans have secured a 'Wei Chi' like advantage over us and must be deemed to be the winner. We shall soon announce our acceptance of Tibetan independence and formally recognise the 'Sovereign Democratic Republic of Tibet'. As to the establishment of diplomatic relations with Tibet, it will take some time before the scars of our surgical separation heal—till then, it should suffice that we recognise the reality of the new State. Our interests in Tibet are many and we shall request some country friendly to both Tibet and China to look after our interests—especially in the matter of many development projects that had been partially completed when the fighting started. So, I hope I have answered your question fully apart from trying to tell you how 'Wei Chi' is played."

"Thank you very much Mr President. You have spared a lot of time for me and I am the wiser for having interacted with you. I shall ask India to pull back its troops soonest possible and definitely by November 1. Thank you again, Mr President. Good night."

"Good Morning to you Mr Starr. Have a great day," Mr Hong said as he poured himself another bowl of Green Tea.

As he lay in his austere 'living' bunker, Mr Hong said to himself, "The conversation with the Secretary General Starr was very useful. I am more hopeful now that we shall be able to achieve 'Peace with Honour'."

Chapter-23

The Road to Peace

Lhasa, Tibet, October 25, 1100 hrs

The first train to arrive at Lhasa Railway Station was a 'Military Special' which had come in from Lanzhou with essential 'Running staff' and was to carry Chinese troops back to Lanzhou. Tibetan functionaries at the station checked out the rake and got it ready for the 27 hour journey to Lanzhou by 1000 hrs. The troops of the former Chinese garrison at Lhasa and some of their families were to travel by this train. Departure of this train was scheduled for 1100 hrs. Three such 'Military Specials' had been arranged by the Chinese to carry back to Lanzhou the troops who had come to capture Lhasa and were in dugouts and make-shift shelters on the eastern side of the town. Town buses had been sent to ferry them to the Railway Station where a 'farewell' high tea had been arranged by the Tibetans for their former 'masters' and 'recent enemies'. The most remarkable thing about the send off given to the departing Chinese was the total absence of hostility on the part of the Tibetans. Initially, the Chinese were nervous and expected shabby treatment but what followed the 'Send Off Tea' was a unique example of Tibetan culture and etiquette.

No 1 Battle Group of Independent Tibetan Army had been detailed to provide a ceremonial 'Honour Guard' to the departing Chinese forces. A few minutes before the train's departure, Commander of the Tibetan Army arrived. The senior PLA Officer—a Colonel—came up to him to bid him Goodbye. However, at his request, the Colonel walked up to the Honour Guard and walked through their ranks. After that, he turned to face the Guard again for their salute. Just then two Tibetan officers with their swords drawn marched up and halted a few paces from him. The Colonel was wondering what was going to happen next. He was totally floored when the Tibetan Commander came up with two men carrying a large tray on which, neatly folded Chinese flags from all over Lhasa had been placed. The Tibetan Commander requested the Chinese officer to accept back the flags of China that flew for 70 years over Lhasa. The two exchanged salutes and the Chinese officer moved to his coach in the train. As the first sound of the engine's horn was heard everyone in the train—all Chinese—looked out to see what the Tibetans on the platform—soldiers and civilians—were doing. Were they celebrating the departure of the Chinese? What they saw will remain in their memory for ever. Every civilian was waving Goodbye while the Honour Guard, still drawn up, presented arms to their former enemy.

Lanzhou, October 26, 1500 hrs

The home-coming of the Chinese first train load was a sombre business to start with. A Brigadier equivalent from the Military Area Command (MAC) had been deputed to receive them along with the representatives of the 21st and 47th Combined Corps whose troops had fought till recently in Tibet. It was a cold, even contemptuous reception that they initially got from the MAC. However, when the Colonel detrained along with two Chinese soldiers carrying the folded Chinese flags, approached the MAC representative and handed over the flags to him, he could see everyone's faces brighten with pride that their boys had brought home their flags from Lhasa. And when they were told about the send-off at Lhasa Railway Station, the Honour Guard, the waving civilians and the ceremonial handing over of the flags, they were totally speechless with amazement. Later that evening on all TV and news channels in PRC a mention of all this was made. After reporting the return of the Chinese personnel from Lhasa, the report made this comment:

> "Our soldiers were sent off from Lhasa with the courtesy and respect which only soldiers feel for their adversaries when they part after battle. It was a magnificent gesture to collect all the Chinese flags and present them back to the Chinese troops as though to say 'You have not been defeated nor have we won'—what actually triumphed at Lhasa was the Code of the Honourable Soldier—and our Tibetan brothers gave a fine example of their courteous culture and spirit."

New Delhi, October 26, 1900 hrs

Chief of Defence Staff met the Prime Minister at 7, Race Course Road after a telephonic conversation with him. General Gyani was intrigued by this summons. On arrival at 7 RCR, he was ushered into the Drawing room of the Prime Minister's residence. He had to wait for just about two minutes before the PM entered.

'Sorry to have to call you up without telling you why. Some matters are better discussed face to face—such is their sensitivity."

General Gyani was completely mystified by this entire 'secrecy' bit. However, other than nodding his head as though in agreement with the PM, he said nothing.

The PM congratulated General Gyani on the very efficient extraction of our troops from various places across the Border with China. He said, "I have spoken with Secretary General Starr and confirmed that there are no Indian troops in China or Tibet. I believe this has been confirmed by Signal/Message also. That is fine as now the Chinese have no reason to continue with their rather menacing Ultimatum. What I wanted to talk to you about was Tibet."

General Gyani was all attention. He knew that one train carrying Chinese troops and families had reached Lanzhou from Lhasa and that three more trains will be on the same duty as announced by Beijing TV and Radio. The PM said, "What I had in mind was the return of His Holiness the Dalai Lama to Tibet. I had spoken to the Speaker of the Tibetan Parliament in Exile and he agreed that we should facilitate the return of His Holiness to his country. Now that the Chinese troops have left and Tibetan troops are looking after Lhasa in all its aspects—virtually like a military Government—I feel we should fly out the Tibetan functionaries in Dharamsala to Lhasa to make arrangements for His Holiness' return. This will include recreating the Tibetan Parliament, the Local Bodies, Police, Posts and Telegraphs, TV/Radio Stations etc and above all getting the Potala Palace refurbished and ensuring suitable buildings are available for the Tibetan Administration to step in and start functioning without delay. He said he would require some help in terms of transportation, carriage of their belongings including Government property to Tibet and in Tibet itself. I have asked him to contact you regarding his requirements. I would suggest you get the Chief Engineer of our Army and practicing experts on various subjects like Communications, Public Relations, TV, Police and so on. You have 'carte blanche' to give the Tibetans anything they ask for or you feel that they may require. In terms of transportation, the Super Hercules aircraft will be very useful for the majority of personnel and stores but His Holiness should be requested to travel by the best aircraft in the VIP Squadron. I am telling you all this because I have already nominated you as our first Ambassador to Tibet, which onerous responsibility, please assume immediately. For the initial rehabilitation of facilities in Lhasa, I have earmarked Rs 200 crore for the present. You may like to meet the Speaker of the Tibetan Parliament who has just arrived at the Gate. Please stay here while I receive him at the portico."

General Gyani thought to himself "We Army people are like 'One Size Fits All' garments! And why not, we Army men can do just about anything!"

The PM entered with the Tibetan Speaker and introduced the CDS and Speaker to each other. "General Gyani—Mr Gyaltsen." The two shook hands formally.

The PM went on "I have nominated General Gyani to be the first Indian Ambassador to Tibet. I have given him a major responsibility in addition to this: he will be responsible to see that the Sovereign Democratic Republic of Tibet functions from the capital Lhasa under as suitable a condition as possible. He will interact with you on virtually every matter regarding Parliament House, office buildings, civilian departments like Police, Power, Trade, Information and so on. He will also help to further consolidate the training of the ITA (Independent Tibetan Army) and assist in bringing into Tibet the benefits of the Information Age and Computers as the driving engine of this age. Movement from India to Tibet will be organised in consultation with you and will be by air. General Gyani will be helped by a team of experts – engineers, information specialists, medical people and a nucleus of the Indian training Team which will organize special training for Independent Tibetan Army personnel and any other force you may decide to raise. I have placed adequate funds at his disposal and more will be provided on demand. Our motive is to see that the 'Snow Lion' Flag flies again over the Potala Palace and Tibet takes its place as the most peaceful member of the UNO."

Mr Gyaltsen bowed in acknowledgement of this speech. "We are indeed fortunate to have India as our neighbour. Buddhism was born here; when we were in dire trouble in the 1950s, India gave us a home for nearly 70 years; and now, again we go back to our land with India's help. May our firm bonds with India become deeper and firmer in the years to come."

General Gyani, every bit the Ambassador Designate said, "Tibet and India are wedded to the culture of peace, tolerance and faith. Now after the closing of the Chinese chapter of Tibetan History, a new chapter opens. Its title will be 'Tibet'. As Ambassador Designate, I shall devote all my energies to make our friendship grow and Tibet regain its pride of place as the most peaceful and tolerant country on Earth."

The PM then escorted both Mr Gyaltsen and the CDS to the portico where their cars were already drawn to take them to their respective residences. Before parting, they exchanged telephone numbers so that it may be easy to coordinate action on any issue as and when the need arises.

General Gyani told Mrs Gyani that he had been posted out again. And before she could say 'Not Again', he said "To Tibet as Ambassador. We go in 7 days."

Chapter-24

The UN Security Council Meets Again

UN Headquarters, New York

November 4, 1000 hrs

The Secretary General, Mr Robert Starr, having confirmed from the belligerents in the recently concluded war that they have pulled back their troops to their own countries, had arranged the meeting of the UNSC on November 4.

The aim of the meeting was to discuss the following issues;-

- The causes of the War.
- Preventive measures that were possible.
- Steps to be taken to avoid occurrence of hostilities specially in a 'Nuclearised' environment.
- Appointment of a Special UN Sub-committee to function under the overall guidance and supervision of the World Bank to review all existing laws pertaining to sharing of waters of 'international' rivers and formulate comprehensive new water laws for the 21st century.

Mr Starr asked Mr Dmitri Pavlov to preside over this important meeting since the Thai member, who was next in line to preside over the meeting had fallen sick and had to be hospitalized.

The Meeting commenced at 1005 hrs.

Opening Address of Mr Dmitri Pavlov, President

We are meeting today under extraordinarily compelling circumstances. Very recently, the two most populous nations of the world confronted each other on a number of battlefields in Asia and in the South China and Arabian Seas. The War climaxed with the threat of turning into the World's First (and probably last) Nuclear War. However, great wisdom and forbearance was displayed by the contending parties and with our indefatigable Secretary General playing a stellar role, a ceasefire and withdrawal of forces to their respective countries, was arranged.

And in the midst of all the nuclear sabre rattling, the Tibetan nation was re-born as the Sovereign Democratic

Republic of Tibet. (Cheers) Sadly the rebirth too was not without bloodshed and a short, sharp war was fought. However, the peace it heralded was marked by great magnanimity, courtesy between the belligerents and total absence of rancour. I am happy to announce on behalf of the Secretary General and the President of the UN General Assembly that Tibet has been granted membership of the United Nations as of this morning. (Cheers) I am also happy to announce that Tibet's admission to the UNO was jointly sponsored by the People's Republic of China and the Republic of India. (Sustained cheering)

Now to the business on hand:

Item 1 – Causes of the War [Notice to speak given only by China and India]

Address by Mr Wang Yuan, Foreign Minister, PRC:

Mr President! I have the honour of stating before this distinguished gathering the causes of this war as perceived by my country.

Foremost cause was India's fomenting of unrest in Tibet, Xinjiang Province and Nei Monggol. The Indian instigation of unrest in Xinjiang was confined to pro-Uyghur separatist propaganda and providing secret support to them in terms of weapons, radio equipment and liaison with Uyghur leaders in their hideouts in the Pamir Heights. To the Nei Monggols, India extended certain additional secret assistance. They, with the help of their agents in the Republic of Mongolia and their National airlines (Air India), arranged free flights for selected commandos and saboteurs from Ulan Bator to New Delhi and thence to Srinagar in Kashmir and back the same way. This activity was generally confined to 6 or 8 people at a time and was for the purpose of imparting commando training and training in fabrication of explosive devices like bombs, explosive grenades, incendiary grenades, IEDs and so on. Though only about 80 Nei Monggol people were trained in Kashmir, they caused great problems to our Government in the resettlement of internally displaced Chinese to areas which were required for some other purpose. On the screen, I shall show a satellite imagery of a camp wantonly burnt to cinders by these persons. I believe some 40 persons perished in that fire which our scientists say was caused by a thermite bomb with some indication of poisonous substances having been used in it. This was found by them by analysis of the wavelengths captured by the satellite image. As far as Tibet is concerned, it is now a free country. However, for over 70 years, India harboured Tibetan refugees who set up a government in Exile, raised an Army and invaded the PRC controlled Tibet to start the war. However, judging by the timing of the Tibetan attack on Lhasa—transported by unmarked but nevertheless distinctly Indian aeroplanes, using Indian parachutes and mainly Indian weapons—we can link this event with the Indian desire to oust PRC from being the Upper Riparian country for the Yarlung Tsangpo and have Tibet in its place. This way, with a friendly Tibet in charge of the 'World's Water Tower' as the Tibetan Plateau is often called, they hoped for more than their share of fresh water from this river and to block any plan PRC may have had for diverting the flow of the river from south to the arid north and North West parts of China. We consider this Indian greed for more water to be the prime cause of what media is already calling 'The Water War'.

Thank you, Mr President and Gentlemen. (Formal clapping)

The Indian Minister for External Affairs then addressed the meeting.

Address by Mr Gambhir Singh Negi, External Affairs Minister, India:

Mr President, I could not believe my years when the

Honourable Mr Wang Yuan ascribed to my country so many skills—all typical of the Underworld's shady characters. In India we cultivate nobler skills like in music and classical dance, like yoga and the poetry of Rabindranath Tagore, skills in Hockey and Kabaddi—all honest civilised activities. We have a great Army, a modern Navy and an Air Force that is our Pride. Our Scientists have sent satellites without number—not only ours but for a great many nations that are our satisfied customers; and our space-craft have landed on the Moon, on Mars and have reached the limits of our Solar System. I confess to all these and a million other achievements. But, we are not murderers; we do not use thermite bombs with a dash of poison as the respected Mr Wang Yuan has alleged. We do support oppressed people everywhere, but only to get their rights in their native lands; we do support free nations that have been long suppressed, their land bespoiled, their faith scoffed at and trampled upon, their population in hundreds of thousands driven out. But not for just one or two days—but for 70-75 years, we have looked after them as our own. And we have the honour to own what is no secret; we armed and trained the Tibetan Patriots who were seeking Freedom for their land, for their Faith and their culture and mores. Yes, when they wished to fight for their cause, we helped them with aircraft, parachutes and the equipment and weapons suited for the righteous Freedom Fighter. All this I confess to. But we are not trying to gain any material advantage like more water from it all! We did all this because our Country and Tibet have a very deep and historical linkage that lives to date. We are the land of Lord Buddha who found enlightenment in our land. We sent no army to Tibet but a son of India—a great Buddhist sage, Sage Padmasambhava, now honoured in all Tibet as Guru Rinpoche who blessed the holiest shrine of Buddhism—the monastery of Pemakochung, alas, now in ruins. But let me not overstate what we did. Doing what we did was our bounden duty—our 'Dharma'.

Why, even today in all the world, India is synonymous with righteousness and good faith, with the abiding conviction that 'as you sow, so shall you reap'. What we sowed were the seeds of good faith and loyalty and what we reaped today is worldwide blessings and in some quarters like in the ruins of Pemakochung monastery, from the shades of Sage Padmasambhava or even the Greatest of all who drew breath, The Buddha Himself (Sustained Cheering)

Mr President, my country did not seek a war; but when an unrighteous action is being perpetrated without let or hindrance at our doorstep, India will pick up the sword to fight the wrong doers. To silently watch the butchery of a people is as much a murder as the butcher's action is. India considers it her moral duty to intervene on behalf of the victim against the aggressor. It is our Dharma. Thank you, Mr President, Gentlemen for the patient listening.

Item 2—Preventive Measures that were Possible
[Notice to speak given only by France and Israel]

Address by M Rene D'Brun, Foreign Minister of France

Monsieur le Presidente, Messieurs. When Honour is endangered, make War to defend it; La France will approve. Where Liberty is threatened, make War to protect it; La France will approve. And when it is but a question of only one litre or one million litres of water—do NOT fight—La France will NOT approve. In the War between India and China, China says it fought because India threatened her dominion over Tibet and helped the Uyghurs and Nei Monggols against oppression. This France believes and approves. China says India waged a war against China in Tibet as that Tibet may give India more water! This is 'tres absurde'—France does not believe this. But both India and China stopped on the brink of the nuclear precipice—

and halted the war. This, France approves. Then what caused the War? Neglect of both great countries to 'talks' and 'meetings' to solve problems as against 'bombs' and breaking of off relations. We live in a violent world. And the tools of violence have changed from the bow and arrow to nuclear and thermonuclear bombs. In such a world, not only those who are fighting suffer but every human being on earth will suffer the effects of a nuclear war. This, France does not approve of. So, *mes ami*, learn to talk to each other if you wish to solve problems; and if you are not able to learn this excellent technique, come to the United Nations to help you break the ice and solve the problem. This is what France wants to convey to this Assembly. Thank You Mr President, thank you Gentlemen. (Sustained Cheering)

Address by Mr David Ben Aaron, Foreign Minister of Israel

Mr President, Gentlemen. The question of War and Peace is eminently debatable. One side is Heads, the other Tails—like a coin. It is such a 50-50 gamble that one wonders if the combatants understand their 'cause' and what they hope to achieve. Let us take the case of China. China hoped to get India off her back as it were. They wanted Tibet to remain a vassal state—in fact, a province of China—forever. By fighting against India, they have lost Tibet forever. Was this what they wished to achieve? Let us see what other option was open to them. China ruled over Tibet for over 70 years without fighting a war. They also did not bother to address the problems that Tibetans faced all these 70 plus years—a subordinate forever. Forever used, never rewarded, culture destroyed, population diluted by transporting Han Chinese into Tibet, religion suppressed, HH the Dalai Lama in exile, the Panchen Lama a Chinese appointee and, in any case, defunct. Is this how you seek to keep a nation—an ancient, self sufficient, cloistered nation like Tibet, under your domination? They had to fail and they did. In Israel, fighting wars has been a feature of our existence. But we fought wars either to survive or to preserve our Nationhood and nation. So, we always won. Is there a lesson for these great countries of the world that seek dominion over others but will not make sure of success by talking to the one they wish to dominate? If they did, there would be no war and both sides could live in peace together. So talk. Thank you Mr President, Gentlemen. (Cheers)

Item3—Avoidance of War in 'Nuclearised' Environment [Notice to speak from the USA only}

Address by Mr John Holt, Vice President of the USA

Mr President, Gentlemen, the recently concluded War between China and India, the two most populous nations of the world and both being significant nuclear powers, gave everyone in the USA and I am sure, in the rest of the World too, nightmares. More than ever, we were close to a nuclear war on October 23 when, after the unilateral declaration of ceasefire by China and her issue of an ultimatum to India to pull back Indian troops from all Chinese territory—this, after China had already pulled back her troops. For a PLAN Flotilla of four ships to be sunk by the IN after the ceasefire had become effective, it was touch and go whether China would react with nuclear weapons or not. However, due to deft handling of the situation by the Secretary General Mr Robert Starr and his rapport with Chinese President Mr Hong, the calamity was averted. India rendered the apology demanded and explained that a communication fault led to the IN ships not being aware of the ceasefire. But, if China had acted rashly, there could have been a very dangerous situation for the whole world.

This brings me to a very vital pre-requisite for

avoidance of war in a nuclearised environment—namely, Communications. If the communications are reliable and have adequate back-ups, vital orders are bound to get through to the intended recipients and war can be averted.

Communications between the leaders of the belligerent countries, or, at least at the Prime Minister/Secretary of State/National Security Advisor level with their counterparts greatly simplifies the process of sorting out very tricky situations like the PLAN-IN encounter on October 23. In fact, though Indian and Chinese leaders did not talk to each other at that time, Mr Starr was able to pacify Mr Hong and persuaded him to settle for an apology. And some world leaders too had a big hand in getting the Chinese President to not take an extreme view of the incident. I need hardly add that but for the fact that the Secretary General and Heads of State of the major countries could speak to the Chinese President, the war may have gone 'very wrong' and not ended in a proper ceasefire as it has.

A leader needs to be a realist and not expect any country he is dealing with to bend over backwards to please him. National Interests are articles of faith for leaders. National Survival is, without question, non-negotiable. If you ask a water stressed nation to give up over 40 per cent of the water carried by a major river, you must be prepared to be pointedly rebuffed. If an unreasonable demand is made on one country, it is up to that country to take a firm stand; if necessary, raise the issue before the UNSC or regional forums or even the International Court of Justice. If, instead of standing up for its rights, a country adopts a compliant doormat like attitude, it should expect more such demands made on it in future.

I would like to make a related point about asymmetrical countries. We have the two classes of countries—the 'Nuclear Haves' and the 'Have Nots'. The latter should be prepared to receive demands that are unreasonable. The best defence for the 'Have Not' is to be very clear about their vital national interests and give no concession whatever relating to them. 'If push comes to shove' appeal to the UN or make another 'Nuclear Have' which is not 'demanding', your ally in resisting the Nuclear 'Bully'. I believe the Bomb is actually unusable in war but can be used to 'bully' a weaker nation—specially one with a weak leader.

One suggestion if I make so bold as to offer is a direct 'lift' from the animal kingdom. In the world of animals, there are predators like Lions, Tigers, Leopards and so on. There are also plenty of animals which can be classified as prey—e.g. deer, antelopes, herbivores generally—though the giants among them can look after themselves quite well. The 'prey' find a degree of safety by living together in herds and protecting the newborns and, if possible, the weak. Predators have to work hard to isolate one animal from the herd to prey on—otherwise, the population of herds will diminish alarmingly. Taking a cue from the animal world, nations which have formed alliances amongst themselves are less vulnerable to being 'preyed' on by 'predator' states. One will recall from history accounts of how alliances help to cool the ardour of the predatory conqueror. In India, the alliance of a large number of small fiefdoms united in an alliance sponsored by the Mauryan King Chandragupta at the instance of the Indian Machiavelli—Chanakya—put a stop to the Eastward advance of Alexander the Great of Greece. Similar alliances in Napoleonic Europe eventually succeeded in defeating Napoleon the Great though they were sorely tried by the great Emperor before they formed their Grand Alliance. In the modern context, alliances such as NATO, SEATO, and CENTO served to deter aggressors from tackling any member of these singly. I am not suggesting that we should emulate the example of NATO and CENTO—perhaps their opponents fell victims to disunity and ceased to be a threat to the likes of NATO. So the old adage 'Unity is Strength' has validity even today and will help discourage predators.

One important suggestion I would like to make to the countries of the World. We need to identify what our vulnerabilities and weaknesses are—these will be the magnets that will attract 'predators'. If we can analyse these and who may be disposed to take advantage of these, we shall have identified the possible 'flash points' in our area. Systematic analysis of this nature will enable nations to establish security systems to keep 'flash points' from flaring up or, better still, defuse them altogether. It is akin to identifying the first cancer cell in one's body and vigorously attacking and destroying it before it becomes a danger to one's life.

With these remarks I conclude my address with a summary of the points I have made—lest in the large number of words I have used, these might get lost:

- Communications must not fail between the Government and the Forces.
- Leaders must keep communication lines open, specially with possible 'predators'.
- Form alliances with like-minded countries.
- If danger threatens, appeal to the UN and strong friends.
- Stay united in your alliance or group.
- Identify the 'flash points' in your area and take steps to defuse them.

Following these simple suggestions will help you from getting involved in hostilities in this nuclearised world. Remember, as the population pressure increases and resources dwindle, new threats will emerge. So, keep a sharp look out for changes that may spell danger for you. Good luck, if you still get involved in a nuclear war!

Thank you Mr President, thank you Gentlemen. (Sustained cheers)

Remarks from Mr Dmitry Pavlov Presiding over the UNSC Session

Gentlemen, we have concluded an useful session in the aftermath of the brief but bitter Sino-Indian War of 2029. We may call it 'The First Water War'. I am not prescient or 'fey' or anything like that. However, I call this 'The First Water War' as the basic reason for the War has not disappeared. It still defies our intelligence and ability to live in peace. The World needs more water every day and the availability of water in the Polar Ice Caps, the Glaciers on our Mountains, the fresh water reservoirs—natural or man-made and the aquifers below the surface of the Earth—all these are slowly but steadily getting depleted. We need to urgently address the question of conserving the available water and eking out the fresh natural supply of water for as long as we can. We need to cut out our lamentable prodigality in wasting fresh water. Our use of this water in agriculture, industry, mining and so on must be controlled. Cropping patterns should be changed so that less water is needed to irrigate our fields; our method of irrigation must be changed so that evaporation losses are minimized; we need to remove polluting industries well away from water sources and water courses; we need to harvest every drop of rain or dew that falls to recharge our aquifers; and we need to find ways of purifying sea water in greater abundance and less cost so as to replace fresh water. These are just a few thoughts about water and its value. I hope we work at it and achieve early results. We shall, if we slow down/control Global Warming.

One last thing which must be mentioned. Like old age that creeps upon us, some of our laws—specially those which regulate the sharing of water of inter-national rivers, need to be revisited and comprehensive new laws for water sharing need to be formulated. The Helsinki Rules, 1966 and the UN Convention of 1977 are over 50 years old and the latter not yet been ratified by UN members concerned! We have to do better than this with our new Law when it is formulated—hopefully within the next three months.

The Secretary General will be issuing the composition of the team that will carry out this task of universal importance by November 11. The future of the World will depend heavily on the work put out by the Team. Good luck to them and to you Gentlemen. I thank you for your patience, cooperation and contributions in the discussion. Thank you. God bless all of us.

Author's Note

The First Water War ended abruptly as the belligerents stood on the edge of the nuclear precipice. We had come to this state in less than two weeks of fighting between China and India! Tens of thousands of soldiers on both sides had lost their lives. In just 45 minutes of a single fire assault with multi-barrelled, long range rocket weapons firing enhanced effect ammunition, over 15,000 soldiers were killed. A few days after this ghastly event, an uneasy cease-fire was called. The belligerents went back to their sides of the international border—all except the countless dead. Was all this bloodshed required? Is this our level of civilization that when sharing of a scarce resource becomes absolutely necessary, we fight and kill each other instead of deciding on a rational way of sharing that resource? Surely what we did was bestial—akin to hyenas around a dead animal! This book aimed at bringing home to its intelligent Readers this important message:

> "Every finite resource will dwindle progressively as the years roll by and human population increases. Sharing and not greedy monopolising is the way of civilized human beings."

The dwindling of resources must be delayed for as long as possible. Prudent usage, search for alternatives, employment of every means of resource conservation and necessary changes of lifestyle—all are required so that we do not come to a crisis situation. We need to remember that 'since the end of the Ice Age 10,000 years ago, melting events have been taking place every 150 years', or so our scientists tell us. Global temperatures have risen by about 1 degree Fahrenheit over the last 100 years; and the rate of warming is increasing steadily. It is recorded that in July 2012, 97 per cent of the ice sheet covering Greenland had melted! Thin ice and 'open' sea water cause more solar energy to be absorbed and lead to more melting. Greenhouse gases that are being generated all the time combined with increased solar energy lead to more melting. So the vicious cycle will go on till we learn to restrict greenhouse gases and set about conservation of the Earth's dwindling water resources—not merely by eliminating wasteful use but also by recharging our planet's drying aquifers. The second message from this book is:

> "Develop by all means but restrict greenhouse gases. Avoid waste of water and recharge the aquifers of our Planet by harvesting rain water and dewfall."

There is great scope for increasing our availability of potable water without depleting natural fresh water resources. The vast seas and oceans that girdle the Earth provide ample scope for the conversion of salt water into potable water by the process of desalination. This is well suited to coastal areas. Costs on the process can be minimised if it is carried out at sea itself and solar energy is used to evaporate sea water and collecting the salt-free vapours of potable water to be piped to the shore. Such a project will cost much less than shore based desalination and also obviate the danger of coast erosion due to giant pipes that return the salty water to sea. It may also be kinder to coastal marine fauna! A project of that nature is already getting ready to start in our southern states. The message we wish to convey in this book is:

> "De-salinate and use sea water instead of using up natural fresh water."

We have also articulated through some of the characters in this book, the need to change our cropping patterns. Rice is a crop that demands copious water supply. Barley is a comparable cereal which is less demanding. A gradual modification of our food habits to include more of Barley and save on rice will help in conserving water. If the acreage devoted to rice cultivation be halved, there will be appreciable saving on water for irrigation. On the subject of irrigation too, the age-old method of open-to-sky water channels carrying water over many kilometres of farmland from the pump house or the canal/distributor, leads to a significant loss of water through evaporation, specially in tropical areas. Laying out a network of robust PVC pipes and use of water sprinklers will be efficient and more economical in the case of most crops that do not need to 'stand' in water. This needs to be explored. There is, too, scope for use of 'hydroponics' or soil-less cultivation of herbs and flowering plants/bushes (also known as 'Bengal System of Gardening). In this system, under controlled conditions of temperature and nutrient supply to individual plants/pots, very little fresh water is used. There is also scope for 'recycling' of waste water after purification purposes as many of our brave space travellers would have experienced. When it becomes necessary, any fluid—be it urine of human or animal origin—if it can be purified to meet human requirements, is a substitute for water! The message here is therefore:

> "Change to crops less demanding in terms of water; go in for more economical methods of watering your farms and orchards—use sprinklers; exploit sea water desalination off shore; examine 'hydroponics' for minimising water expenditure; and recycle waste water."

In this book, the liberation of Tibet has been given great importance. The conquest of Tibet by China, the flight of the 'Khampas' and the subsequent decades of Chinese rule over Tibet have never been accepted by the helpless Tibetan. He, therefore, is often reduced to commit self-immolation. A regime which is so brutal and concentrates on the extinction of the Tibetan race and culture must not be allowed to carry out its reprehensible programmes unchecked. We, therefore, put up a resurgent India to champion Tibet's cause and enabled her to recapture the capital Lhasa unaided and regain control over the rest of Tibet with the help of the Indian Army. Many would call the Indian support to question, term it as interference in China's affairs and so on. We are content that what we achieved for Bangladesh against misrule by Pakistan, we were able to replicate for Tibet against misrule by China. It is not a matter for legal quibbling; it was the demand of everything humanity stands for—human rights, self rule and freedom to live one's own traditional way of life. What we wish to leave as a message for today's 'colonists and enslavers' is this:

> "Human Rights are not negotiable. Any infringement of these will attract retribution. Sooner or later, the enslaver and exploiter will hit the dust. And not all

> enslaved and newly liberated people will display the kind of nobility that the Tibetans did; another may dishonour your soldiers, your Flag and take up arms against such of your countrymen as are still staying in the newly liberated land. The Tibetans are a people of great refinement; they let their tormentors go with honour."

There are other oppressed peoples who have been brought into the book peripherally. Our purpose was to indicate by a few incidents the manner in which oppressed people might fight for their rights. The Uyghurs, an Islamic people, do not accept their subordination to a God-less state. They can and will rebel against perceived and demonstrated injustices. By a different token, Southern Mongolia, which, as the name suggests, should have been handed over to the Republic of Mongolia by the Russians in 1950, is treated as a colony by the Chinese government. Its pastures are increasingly becoming settlements for China's burgeoning population. It is very likely that, like the Great Genghis Khan, another leader may take a poor view of the situation as it stands and initiate vigorous measures to free his country. The message for the People's Republic of China is, therefore:

> "Do not be unjust with your minority population. Do not treat those whose lands you have been 'given' by mistake as slaves and their lands as dumping areas for your surplus population. The worm will turn one day."

The final issue that has been highlighted in this book is the question of nuclear war. Chapter 21 (The President Decides) and the vote of the majority of the 300 Party Members consulted by President Hong, suggest that nuclear war is un-thinkable for the majority of Chinese people. One would expect this pattern of voting from every section of this ancient Civilisation. Mass annihilation does not form any part of Chinese culture and we, therefore, took a poll on this vital issue, courtesy President Hong. The message that emerges is that:

> "Civilizational or Race Memory plays a far greater part in an ancient and great Nation's decision-making process than the political theories and practices acquired from alien nations that appear to have forsaken their inherited wisdom and are a danger to human civilization. China, happily for all of us, is NOT one of them in this respect."

To write 'Finis' to this book, as its author, I hope the messages I have culled out for your ready reference in this note will serve as a guide in times to come.

Bibliography

1. *Water: Asia's New Battle Ground* by Brahma Chellaney; Harper Collins Publishers, India—a JV with The India Today Group, New Delhi: 2011.
2. *Interpreting China's Grand Strategy – Past, Present and the Future* by Michael D Swaine and Ashley J Tellis; Published by RAND: 2000.
3. *On China* by Henry A Kissinger; Penguin Group: 2011-2012.
4. *China's Splendours;* China Travels and Tourism Press.
5. *Breakout Nations* by Ruchir Sharma; Allen Lane, Penguin Group: 2012.

6. *Indian Explorers of the 19th Century* by Indra Singh Rawat; Publications Division Ministry of Information and Broadcasting, New Delhi: June 1973.
7. *Riddle of the Tsangpo Gorges* by Francis Kingdon Ward; Published by Edward Arnold & Co. Republished by Antique Collectors Club: April 2005.
8. *Tsangpo: The Final Exploration* by Harish Kapadia; Published 2005/Source Himalayan Journal 61 (http. www.himalayanclub.org/journal/tsangpo-the-final-exploration)
9. *USI Journals* April-June 2012: Jan-Mar 2013: Apr-Jun 2013.
10. *CLAWS Journal* Winter 2009: Autumn 2010: Spring 2011 & Summer 2013.

General & Military Info on China: Question Bank

Historical/Political/General

Q1. When was the People's Republic established in China?

Ans. The year 1949.

Q2. When did China occupy Tibet?

Ans. The Year 1950.

Q3. What major war occurred between India and China and other incidents of confrontation?

Ans. Sino-Indian Conflict, October, 1962; Nathula Clash 1967; Wang Dung Stand-Off, 1986.

Q4. What are China's territorial claims against India?

Ans. China's major claims of Indian territory are:

a. Aksai Chin (Ladakh) – 38,000 sq km

b. Arunachal Pradesh (China calls it South Tibet) – 96,000 sq km

Q5. What are the on-going measures to solve the border disputes and to maintain peace on the line of actual control?

Ans.

a. Regular meetings of Joint Working Group & Experts Group – over 15 meetings held.

b. Exchange of maps for Uttarkhand – HP borders with Tibet.

c. Signing of Border Peace and Tranquillity Agreement, 1993.

d. Agreement on Confidence Building Measures in the Military Field, 1996

Q6. Who are our neighbours with whom China is very friendly?

Ans. Pakistan and Myanmar.

Q7. Which countries of Asia is China trying to cultivate around India?

Ans. Sri Lanka, Nepal, Maldives

Q8. What is India's worry in relation to river Brahmaputra?

Ans. India's worry relates to the Chinese plan to divert the flow of the Brahmaputra river at the Great Bend near which it enters India and make it flow Northwards to North and NW China. This, if done will deprive the Ganges of over 30 per cent of its water, adversely affect agriculture, flora and fauna along the entire course of the river. It will also affect Bangladesh, reduce the size of the Delta and cause sea water to infiltrate into the dry river bed banks.

Q9. When did the 'China-India Strategic Dialogue' start? What has been achieved so far? Is strategic

partnership achievable or increased cooperation the limit—at least for the present?

Ans. *On April 11, 2005, the Prime Minister of India and China (Dr. Manmohan Singh and Mr Wen Jiabao) announced a new 'Strategic and Cooperative Partnership'. Since then cooperation has increased between the two countries, e.g. in the Doha WTO negotiations, on environment issues in the Copenhagen World Climate Summit, 2009; in the Hand-in-Hand series of joint military exercises at Kunming in 2007 and Belgaum in 2008. So far, while cooperation has increased, strategic partnership has been entirely elusive though five rounds of talks have taken place.*

Q10. What are the boundary disputes China has with its neighbours (other than India)?

Ans. *China had/has border disputes with countries other than India. Most of these are about small tracts of land close to their borders with those countries. Such disputes involved North Korea, Mongolia, Kazakhstan, Kyrgyztan, Tajikistan, Vietnam, Russia, Myanmar and Bhutan, with Vietnam, China also has disputes regarding Spratley Islands in South China Sea and Paracel Islands in the Gulf of Tonkin.*

Q11. Who are the President and Prime Minister of China?

Ans. *President: Xi Jinping; Prime Minister: Li Kequiang.*

Q12. Who has been often called 'The Great Helmsman'?

Ans. *Late Chairman Mao Zedong.*

Q13. Which country held the 2008 Olympic Games?

Ans. *People's Republic of China.*

Military

Q14. How are the armed forces of China called?

Ans. *People's Liberation Army (PLAA, PLAN, PLAAF)*

Q15. Who has absolute leadership over the armed forces, in principle?

Ans. *Absolute Leadership vests in The Communist Party of China.*

Q16. In practice, which body actually carries out the task of supreme military leadership?

Ans. This is done by Central Military Commission (CMC) established jointly by the Communist Party and the State (Govt).

Q17. Does the PLA Report to the Chinese State Council (Government) or to the two Central Military Commissions (CMCs), one set up by the State and another by the Party?

Ans. PLA does not report to the State Council (Govt). It reports to the two CMCs.

Q18. Who constitute the CMC?

Ans. CMC is composed as under:

a) Chairman – Gen Secy of the Chinese Communist Party
b) Vice Chairmen – 2 – both Generals.
c) Members – Minister of National Defence (General)
Chief of General Staff of PLA (do)
Director, General Political Dept (do)
Director General Logistics Dept (do)

Q19. What are the departments that constitute the PLA General Headquarters?

Ans. PLA General Headquarters has four departments. These are:

a) General Staff Dept (GSD)
b) General Political Dept (GPD)
c) General Logistic Dept (GLD)
d) General Armament Dept (GAD) also called GED

Q20. What are the Military Regions under the General Staff HQ?

Ans. The following are the military regions under GSHQ:

a) Shenyang Military Region
b) Beijing Military Region
c) Langzhou Military Region
d) Jinan Military Region
e) Nanjing Military Region

f) Guangzhou Military Region (also administers the PLA at Hong Kong & Macau)
g) Chengdu Military Region

Q21. How is Loyalty to the Party and Civilian Government ensured?

Ans. *The GPD maintains a system of Political Commissars, which maintain separate chain of command to ensure loyalty to the Party and to the civilian Government.*

Q22. What are the Service Branches of The Chinese Armed Forces?

Ans. *The following are the service Branches of The Chinese armed Forces:*
a) PLA Ground Force (PLAA)
b) PLA Navy (PLAN)
c) PLA Air Force (PLAAF)
d) Second Artillery Corps (SAC)

Q23. What are the functions of the General Staff Department?

Ans. *GSD carries out staff and operational functions for the PLA and has major responsibility for implementation of plans. Headed by Chief of General Staff it serves as HQ for the ground forces and contains directorates of the Air Force, Navy and Strategic Missile Force.*

Q24. How is Military Intelligence organized in China?

Ans. *Military Intelligence at the central level is composed of the Second and Third Department of PLAGHQ, and the Liaison Dept under PLA GPD.*

At all military regions Second Bureau, on par with operations department, is responsible for intelligence.

The Third Department of the PLA controls all communication stations in the garrison area of all military regions.

Q25. What is the Second Artillery Corps (SAC)? What is it's strength, organisation, weapon holdings and

delivery means?

Ans. *Second Artillery Corps (SAC) is the strategic missile force of the PLA. It controls both nuclear and conventional strategic missiles. China is estimated to have between 100-400 nuclear weapons. SAC has 90,000 to 120,000 personnel and six ballistic missile divisions (Missile Corps Bases) The six divisions are deployed independently in different military regions and have a total of 15 to 20 missile brigades.*

Q26. What are China's Special Forces called nowadays? What are their capabilities?

Ans. *Chinese Special Forces are called 'Immediate Action Unit (IAU). A large number of IAUs are drawn from PLAA. They deal with all terrorist activity within China. They have also reportedly developed a force under Guangzhou Military Region nicknamed 'Sword of Southern China'. They consist of highly intelligent and educated personnel trained to respond to any contingency by air or by sea. They are regarded as versatile fighters.*

Q27. What are the capabilities of Chinese Information operations?

Ans. *Their main task is 'Cyber Spying', 'Hacking' and 'Cyber Security'*

PLAN

Q28. What are the Fleets into which PLAN is organized?

Ans. *PLAN is divided into three fleets:*

a. *North Sea Fleet – HQ Qingdao in Shandong Province*
b. *East Sea Fleet – HQ Ningo in Zhejiang Province*
c. *South Sea Fleet – HQ Zhanjiang in Guangdong Province*

Q29. What does each Fleet consist of?

Ans. *Each fleet has surface forces (Destroyers, Frigates, amphibious vessels etc), submarine forces, Coastal defence units and aircraft.*

Q30. What are the main Naval Bases including Nuclear Sub-Marine Base?

Ans. *Main Naval bases are Qingdao, Dinghai and Zhan Jiang. Nuclear Submarine base is coming up near Sanya (Hainan Island) and could hide up to 20 nuclear submarines.*

PLAAF

Q31. What are the Military Region Air Forces (MRAF)?

Ans. *These are Beijing, Lanzhou, Chengdu, Nanjing, Shenyang and Jinan Military Region Air Force (MRAF). In addition PLAAF Airborne forces have 2 airborne corps and 2 airborne divisions.*

Q32. How many air bases are utilised by PLAAF in the seven military regions?

Ans. *Over 150 air bases are used by PLAAF – these are divided among the seven military regions.*

Q33. What are the approximate holdings of aircraft in the PLAAF?

Ans. *Over 1300 Aircraft all types.*

Q34. What are the approximate holdings of vessels in the PLAN?

Ans. *Air Craft Carrier, 26 Destroyers, 45 Frigates, 69 Submarines (13 are nuclear powered), 9 Corvettes,122 Missile Boats, 231 Patrol vessels, 107 Mine countermeasure vessels, 5 Replenishment oilers, 3 Docks and number of auxiliary smaller vessels.*

Q35. What is the disposition of the PLA in various military regions?

Ans. *Each Military Region has a Group Army with varying numbers of infantry/armoured/mechanized divisions, infantry/armoured/mechanised/artillery/AAA/Air Defence brigades and specialised regiments like engineers/signals/Chemical Defence/Electronic Warfare/Bridging/Helicopters. The Group armies are 27th, 38th and 65th in*

Beijing MR, 16th, 39th and 40th in Shenjang MR, 21st, 47th and Xinjiang Military District in Lanzhou MR, 20th, 26th and 54th in Jinan MR, 1st, 12th and 31st in Nanjing MR, 41st and 42nd in Guangzhou MR and 13th, 14th and Tibet Military District in Chengdu MR.

Defence Budget

Q36. What is the Chinese Defence Budget for 2014-15 and by how much has it increased since last financial Year?

Ans. Chinese Defence Budget for 2014-15 is $ 132 bn representing a 12.2 per cent increase over the previous year. In comparison, India's Defence Budget is a quarter of the Chinese Def Budget – approximately $ 33 bn.

Q37. In which area is Chinese Maritime Movement most Vulnerable?

Ans. Chinese Maritime Movement is most vulnerable in the general area of Malacca Straits.

Index